You Can Almost Take It with You

Commonsense Investing and Estate Planning

▮

by Edwin C. Anderson

David S. Lake Publishers
Belmont, California

ISBN 0-8224-9893-6
Library of Congress Catalog Card Number: 86-82791
Printed in the United States of America
1. 9 8 7 6 5 4 3 2 1

Contents

DEDICATION

To my wife, Jeanne, and in memory of my mother, Josephine. For a love given, a life shared. The only true wealth, the only lasting inheritance.

▎■▏

ACKNOWLEDGMENTS

He said, "To make a long story short . . ." His listener interrupted, "Too late."

It may now indeed be too late to express my gratitude for the patience and forbearance of my family, friends, law partners, clients, former classmates, acquaintances, and, on occasion, total strangers, who listened in stunned silence as I seized the slightest opportunity to relate the saga of writing this book. And if my gratitude is not too late, I am sure it is too little.'

To Bob Barrett, National Associates, Inc., Pension Consultants, Betty Bartley and her husband Chuck (who is writing a book titled *Never Go Skiing with a Guy Who's Writing a Book*); Jim and Sandy Codding; the Honorable Ferdinand F. Fernandez, judge of the federal district court; Kathie Gann; June Grubschmidt; John P. Harris, attorney, Seattle; Kathleen Hartley; Connie Hinch; D. Ford Howe, attorney, San Francisco; Bill Hutchinson, investment advisor, Shuman, Schneider & Hutchinson, San Francisco; Jim Jordan, Jordan & Andrews, actuaries, Santa Rosa, California; Olive Kerr; Meryl King; Hugh Levin; Ed Pisenti, CPA; Sparky Schulz; Diane Trembley; Dr. Fred Wessa; and Leslie Wilson—my appreciation for their encouragement and constructive comments on the manuscript.

And a special thanks to my law partners, Kirt F. Zeigler, Rob Disharoon, Jerry Gray, and Barbara Detrich, for their faith and help in keeping me on track.

Thanks also to my agent, Brad Bunnin, for his willing ear and wise counsel, and to Gloria Frym, Joseph A. Rattigan, retired California appellate court justice, and Sylvia E. Stein for their excellent editorial work and for making this a better book.

And most especially I thank Betty Stone, a semiretired secretary in our office. Not only did she give up many weekends (even missing Sunday football) to type the manuscript, but she provided many insights and suggestions that were most helpful. She is a true friend, and I hope "our book" meets her expectations.

Making Decisions

When John F. Kennedy was elected the thirty-fifth president of the United States, he inherited from his predecessor, President Eisenhower, a plan to train fourteen hundred anti-Castro exiles to invade Cuba and overthrow the Castro government.

At first Kennedy had serious doubts about the execution and political repercussions of such a plan. However, he was assured of the plan's success by the Joint Chiefs of Staff, the secretary of state, the secretary of defense, the head of the CIA, and each member of his cabinet.

The invasion was a disaster. The plan was poorly conceived. The president of the United States had been misinformed and had acted on poor advice. And a wiser president was made acutely aware of his responsibility.

The decision-making process is making choices. We rely on our knowledge, our experience, and the advice of others; but the final decision is a test of our judgment. We often don't perceive that relying on someone else's opinion does not relieve us of the responsibility for the consequences of our decisions.

A number of highly paid athletes and other newsworthy celebrities, relying on their investment advisors, have made bad investments that left many of them bankrupt and with outstanding tax liabilities. Millions of other Americans have done the same. The tragedy of those who make poor investments is not only that they have lost their money, but that they have passed up the opportunity to make sensible and prudent investments that would provide financial security for them and their families.

Most people believe that investment and estate planning is complicated, technical, and for the most part beyond their comprehension and that the success of their plans depends on finding some all-knowing investment and estate planner in whom they can put their faith and trust. It is true that you will rely on the advice and recommendations of professionals in the fields of estate and investment planning, if only to confirm your own thinking. You will also rely on professionals for tax planning and for preparing legal documents. You do need advice, and you do need constructive suggestions.

However, the plan required for your financial security and for the disposition of your assets upon death is far too important to leave entirely to experts. You choose the advisors on whom you rely. You define the objectives and set the priorities for your investments. And although you may need guidance and direction, your actions must, above all, reflect your feelings, your attitudes, and your philosophy. Only by understanding and accepting your role in the control and development of your investment and estate plan can you be assured that your objectives will be accomplished.

This book is about that role.

PART I

∎

Investment Planning

A lopsided man runs fastest
Along the little sidehills of success.
Frank Moore Colby
(provided by Charles M. Schulz)

CHAPTER 1

Investing: The Great Secret

If only foolproof methods of investing had been developed, two things are certain: the founder would not have shared the secret in return for a newsletter fee, the price of a book, or brokerage commissions; and had he done so, the perfect system would have collapsed as investors adjusted to the information.

John C. Boland,
Wall Street Insiders

Most people think that if you want to make investments or plan your estate, you simply find a good investment advisor or a qualified estate planner. But if you rely solely on the advice of an advisor, you'll be like the woman who gave up her family, her home, and her career to go in search of her guru. After several difficult and frustrating years, she finally found him on a mountaintop in Nepal. Exhausted, but delighted with her good fortune, she told him, "I have given up everything to come in search of you. I cannot tell you how much this means to me. Please, tell me, what is the great secret of life?"

After a pause he responded, "Life is like a flowing river."

Puzzled, she asked, "What does that mean?"

Shrugging his shoulders, he answered, "Okay, so life isn't like a flowing river."

There are many such "gurus" who provide investment and estate-planning advice. They pretend to possess a knowledge about the future that none can hold. The "great secret" is that no one really knows whether interest rates in the next six months will rise (as many qualified advisors predict) or fall (as many qualified advisors predict). No one knows whether the economy will thrive—with increased business activity, a low rate of inflation, and reduced energy costs—or whether the economy will be ravaged by a recession or depression. It is extremely difficult, if not impossible, to predict with any degree of accuracy the height, depth, and length of inflations, depressions, and other changes in the economy. It is even more difficult to foresee the impact of these changes on any category of investments and on any particular investment within that category.

Even the most knowledgeable experts aren't infallible. For example, a Nobel prize–winning economist told the President's Council of Economic Advisors in the 1960s that anyone who did not protect himself by buying equities (common stocks) was so stupid that he deserved to lose his wealth. Although the economist's conclusions appeared reasonable at the time, those who followed this advice saw their wealth decrease in value and purchasing power during the next fifteen years as a result of higher inflation (as foreseen by the economist) and a corresponding and unpredictable decrease (unforeseen by anyone) in common stock values during this same period.

Venita Van Caspel, a nationally known financial planner, called inflation "the Robin Hood of the 1970s" and predicted that it will continue to be the Super Robin Hood of the 1980s. The jacket of her book, *Money Dynamics for the 80's,* promises that the reader can cope with the special money problems of the 1980s and achieve financial security and independence.

She recommended the purchase of hard assets such as real property, diamonds, gold, and oil. (These are properties that are expected to increase in value during times of hyperinflation and that had performed well during the 1970s.) She saw no chance that the rate of inflation would fall in the next decade.

Van Caspel also recommended the purchase of a mutual fund holding shares in companies that had invested in South African gold mining operations, stating that, "Those clients [of hers] who responded to [this] recommendation in 1979 were rewarded with a 235% gain in a year's time." When she gave this advice, gold was trading at approximately $810 an ounce. The price of gold continued to rise and reached an all-time high of $875 an ounce by mid-1980. Then gold began to decline in value. By June of 1982 gold was selling at $300 an ounce.

Finally, Van Caspel recommended investments in oil and gas limited partnerships, noting that these had the advantage of owning a product that "everyone wants, everyone needs, and is in short supply." Amazingly and to everyone's surprise, the price of oil declined in value from its 1980 highs, and by the mid-1980s there was an "oil glut."

As you can see, even Van Caspel had difficulty pointing out the kinds of investments that would produce financial security and independence.

Even investment strategies attuned to short time frames face uncertainty and surprises. For example, an article on interest rates in the July 2, 1984, *Wall Street Journal* concluded that most analysts participating in a newspaper survey predicted higher interest rates over the next six months and further increases in interest in the first half of 1985. On the day the article was published, the interest from treasury bonds provided a 13.9 percent rate of return. Within sixty days, the interest rate on these bonds had dropped to less than 12.5 percent. Interest rates then declined further during 1985 and continued to do so in the first part of 1986.

Why is it impossible for anyone to predict with consistency where your money should be invested and which particular investment or group of investments—such as stocks, bonds, or real property—will increase in value? Investment predictions are based on expectations that the economy will respond favorably or unfavorably during a given period. The belief that interest rates will rise or fall, that inflation will remain low, or that employment figures will increase or decrease will directly affect the demand for one particular category of investment over another.

But regardless of the soundness of the premises on which these predictions are based, how thoroughly they are analyzed, and the number of experts who concur with the answers, the assumptions will often prove erroneous because of events— political, military, human, natural—that are simply beyond anyone's control and thus cannot be foreseen. Even if the economy continued in the direction predicted, the anticipated impact upon a particular investment may not take place because, as we have seen, other events in the marketplace also affect that investment's value.

THE ECONOMISTS

Predictions regarding the future of the economy are not made by investors, as you might assume, but rather by economists. Economists are knowledgeable about the economic history of the major civilizations, and they construct theories about why the economies of these civilizations prospered or failed. Armed with this knowledge and their interpretations of history, they publish books, articles, and newsletters predicting the future of the economy. Governmental agencies, financial institutions, corporations, and individuals, all part of the investing public, rely on their theories and opinions.

The near bankrupt state of many such agencies and institutions is due, at least in part, to a naive trust in the ability of economists to accurately predict the future direction of the economy and its impact on particular investments. Even economists themselves wonder about their powers. As the late Frank H. Knight said in an address before the American Economic Association in 1951, "I have been increasingly moved to wonder whether my job is a job or a racket, whether economists . . . should cover their faces or burst into laughter when they meet on the street."

During his term in office, President Jimmy Carter invited small groups of recognized experts in many fields to discuss with him various issues confronting his administration. This group included governors, members of Congress, business executives, labor leaders, economists, and energy experts. In his memoirs, *Keeping Faith,* President Carter commented that, for the most part, he found these discussions helpful. He indicated, however, one notable exception, "The [meeting] with the economists was a waste of time; they all expounded their own conflicting theories and seemed to be unwilling or unable to consider the views of others or deal in a practical way with the economic problems I was having to face every day."

GAMBLING VERSUS INVESTING

If no one really knows, then isn't investing simply a matter of luck—of being in the right place at the right time? Isn't it all just a big gamble?

When we watch the news on television and see the individual who bought a lottery ticket for $1 and won millions, we can hardly argue that luck does not have its place. But, in fact, the lottery winner didn't invest at all. He gambled. He gambled and he won. There is a thin but very real line between investing and gambling, and it only becomes blurred in retrospect. Investors are not guaranteed success; they do suffer losses. Gamblers do not always lose; sometimes they get lucky.

A principal difference between investing and gambling is in the attitude we take when our money is committed. When we gamble our money, we are prepared to lose—and most of the time we do. Millions of people who bought lottery tickets and watched the winners hold up their checks never really expected to walk away rich. When we invest, we do not expect to lose our investment; we expect income and appreciation. At the very least, we expect our money back.

To gamble is a personal choice. To invest is a personal choice. Unfortunately, many people believe they are investing when they are gambling—often at incredibly poor odds. You are gambling when you commit your money with the attitude that there are quick and easy profits to be made and that someone is going to take your money and put it into investments he or she knows will make you wealthy. Benjamin Graham, author of *The Intelligent Investor*, best described this subtle but significant distinction between investor and gambler when he wrote, "The further one gets from Wall Street, the more skepticism one will find, we believe, as to the pretensions of stock market forecasting or timing. The investor can scarcely take seriously the innumerable predictions which appear almost daily and are his for the asking. It is absurd to think that the general public can ever make money out of market forecasts."

THE PROBLEM IN SELECTING INVESTMENT ADVISORS

If attempting to predict the future of the economy is not a sound basis for an investment strategy, can you simply go out and find yourself a good investment advisor? Not likely. Competent investment advisors are greatly outnumbered by those who purport to be investment advisors but who have limited knowledge and whose real objective is to promote particular investments. Thus, they are salespeople first and investment advisors only to the extent that it promotes their product.

These purported advisors frequently recommend ways to save on taxes, and we are enticed by any investment that offers a tax-saving opportunity. These *tax shelters* can accompany the acquisition of virtually any asset. Tax shelters and investments are promoted by stockbrokers, insurance salespeople, financial planners, financial consultants—anyone claiming to be qualified to provide financial and investment advice. Some of the most respected corporations in America also promote financial planning and the sale of financial products. These financial promoters gain your confidence through advertising and seminars promoting their investments. The result: the investing public, which believes it is getting investment advice, is in fact getting investment promotion.

Financial planners even hold classes at accredited institutions of higher learning. During one semester at a local community college, at least eighteen courses were offered on the subjects of tax, investment, and estate planning. Even here investors are often not receiving objective investment advice but rather attempts to motivate them to become clients and to purchase investment products.

Such courses often promise too much and deliver little but biased advice. One example was a two-session program entitled, "How to Invest Like the Big Guys (Secret: Limited Partnerships)." The course description promised to provide "all you need to know about oil and gas, real estate, collectibles, research and development, agribusiness, and equipment leasing." It is "all you need to know" to prove the truth of the saying that, "A fool and his money are soon parted."

Financial planners direct much of their promotion toward the small investor because of the tremendous sums now invested in IRA and Keogh accounts. But even if you are wealthy, finding a qualified investment advisor who understands your objectives is extremely difficult. This problem was demonstrated by the complaints of four women whose stories were published in an article in the *San Francisco Chronicle* entitled "Rich Women Who Are Fighting Back." All capable and intelligent individuals, these women had three things in common: (1) They owned substantial wealth. (2) Their wealth was managed for them by professionals. (3) They were frustrated by the results.

Iris Love, a descendant of the Guggenheims, was a beneficiary of three trusts established by her grandmother and administered by a trust company. She is quoted as saying, "I have always felt their attitude was looking down on me, perhaps because I am a woman, and I am not supposed to know anything at all about the world of finance." She added, "My grandmother would be appalled at what they've done."

Mrs. Wendy Lehman, beneficiary of a large Vanderbilt family trust, sued the trust company managing her mother's trust because of excessive fees charged against the trust. She ultimately prevailed, but only after lengthy and expensive litigation.

The Austrian Countess de Rachevsky had nothing good to say about her financial advisor and was quoted as "steaming" about the investment advice she had received from her brokerage firm.

Mrs. Tony Webb, widow of millionaire builder and former owner of the Yankees Del Webb, alleged that she lost $625,000 when her investment advisor and her broker pledged her tax-free bonds as collateral for highly speculative stock options, which became worthless when the market did not perform as expected. She sued her investment advisor, her broker, and her brokerage firm and recovered $418,000 in damages. Her advice to every person establishing a trust or retaining a financial advisor was, "Never allow anyone to do anything you don't understand with your money."

Mrs. Webb gives excellent advice. When you don't actively participate in investing your money, you can be taken for a ride, no matter how rich you are. The *Wall Street Journal* shed further light on this subject in an article entitled "Big Increase in Investment Products Creates Problems for Brokers, Clients." The article stated,

> Proliferation of products from stock index options to tax shelters created problems both for brokers in keeping current and for their clients who purchased these assets on the assumption that the broker's knowledge about them is much greater than, in fact, it is. . . . Even though they may not fully understand the risks and rewards of these new products, brokers tend to push them either because they carry high commissions or because aggressive product managers are applying pressure.

Learn from these illustrations the importance of knowing the "great secret." Take control of your money decisions. Take responsibility for your own security and well-being.

DEVELOPING AN INVESTMENT STRATEGY

What are the first steps in developing a sound investment strategy? Initially, recognize that you have an investment strategy whether or not you have consciously adopted one. You invest your money when you keep it in a bank account because it is safe. You invest your money when you use it to purchase common stocks because you feel that they will increase in value. When you give your money to someone promoting an investment on the promise that it will increase in value, this, too, reflects your investment strategy.

The first step to being a good investor is to avoid being a bad investor. Good investors have a conscious set of criteria that each investment must meet. Bad investors have no such criteria; they believe they can rely on their instincts and knowledge of people to make wise investments. Good investors control their emotions when making investment decisions. They are realistic, and they pay attention to their doubts. If they doubt the wisdom of a particular investment or if they are not satisfied that it is consistent with their objectives, good investors forego an opportunity that may later turn out to have been a sound investment. Their standards for making an investment must be met. They have learned the folly of haste and the wisdom of patience.

Good investment planning and good estate planning, like good writing, are best when kept simple and direct. All three must be understandable. Good investors learn the importance of attitude and approach in developing a successful investment strategy.

Ted Williams, perhaps baseball's greatest natural hitter and the holder of many records, was once asked his proudest achievement. His surprising answer, "Most bases on balls." When asked why he valued this record, he said, "Because it proved that I had the patience and discipline to wait for the right pitch."

Good investors don't rely on wishful thinking. They get the facts. And they have the patience to wait for the right pitch.

CHAPTER 2

Taking Control

*I have but one lamp by which my feet are guided
and that is the lamp of experience.*

Patrick Henry

Two losers were sitting on a park bench discussing their sad plight when one asked the other, "What happened to you?" The other responded, "I wouldn't listen to anybody. How about you?" "I listened to everybody," came the reply.

Many of us share these feelings and frustrations as we review our investment decisions. Experienced investors know that they are most responsible for the success or failure of their investments and that they alone will reap the rewards and bear the losses. They must become informed. They must take control.

Your investment choices range from the traditional (such as stocks, bonds, money market funds, real property, gold and silver) to the esoteric (race horses, sailboats, stamps, antiques, commodities futures, stock options). You can invest by purchasing one of these assets or by acquiring an interest in a limited partnership or mutual fund that owns one or more of them. Stockbrokers, insurance companies, and financial planners who promote such investment products often rate them from "safe" or "relatively safe" to "risky" or "very risky." Promoters tell us that the potential for reward is directly related to our willingness to be aggressive in assuming risk—that is, to acquire speculative investments.

UNDERSTANDING RISK

Every investment involves two risks: an *investment risk* and a *market risk*. Investment risk relates to the quality of the investment as compared to other investment choices. In other words, does this investment present a greater risk of your principal—your investment—than other similar assets?

For example, the relationship between the security of your principal and the interest you receive on a bond is determined by your willingness to assume an investment risk. You can invest your money in a bank account or treasury bill secured by the federal government and receive less interest. Or, you can invest your money in a deed of trust secured by real property or loan your money to someone who has less financial responsibility than the federal government, and you will receive a higher rate of interest. You are receiving this higher interest because your principal is not as secure as it would be if its repayment were guaranteed by the federal government. The risk is inherent in the investment itself.

Market risk is a separate factor in every investment choice. It is the risk of inflation, depression, war, or drought. It is the risk of unforeseen and unanticipated world and national events that have a direct impact—some favorable, some unfavorable—on the economy and your investment.

Market risk is best demonstrated by a review of the most common investment choices during the past fifty years and how they responded to changes in the economy during this period. Neither the depth nor the length of the Great Depression was anticipated by those who made investments in the late 1920s. During the depression years from 1930 to 1941, both common stocks and real property declined in value from their high in the late 1920s.

Those who borrowed to invest in these assets with expectations of an increase in market value (quick profits) discovered the harsh realities of attempting to project the future direction of the economy. When the depression struck, many of these investors who had purchased assets with borrowed money discovered that the amounts they owed exceeded the fair market value of their assets. When the values of these assets dropped dramatically, as in the case of common stocks, the debt obligations remained. Because the market value of both stocks and real property dropped simultaneously, many of these investors quickly discovered that the total market value of all their assets was less than their obligations. This is why many individuals during the late 1920s and early 1930s lost their entire wealth to creditors and to bankruptcy. For many, the result was a financial disaster of the greatest magnitude.

A large-scale economic recovery marked the twenty-year period following the Second World War. It brought unprecedented prosperity to millions of Americans. It was a golden age for investors—a period of low inflation, low energy costs, and high productivity. The economy was fueled by the pent-up demands of a new generation committed to a higher standard of living. The stock market thrived. Real property values increased.

Real property, traditionally purchased with borrowed money, continued to increase in value during the postwar period. Stocks of the blue chip companies of American industry also continued to rise. Those who borrowed against real property and stock holdings to acquire more of these assets continued to reap the harvest of a strong and dynamic economy. Their net worths skyrocketed. Those who owned bonds, particularly long-term bonds, and those who kept their cash in bank accounts at low interest rates saw the market value of their bonds and the purchasing power of their cash decline as stocks and real property increased in value.

A constantly rising inflation rate marked the period from the late 1960s through the 1970s. The results were rising costs and abnormally high interest rates. Real property and other hard assets—such as timber, oil, gold, silver, diamonds, works of art, antiques, and stamps—appreciated in value during this period. Due to investor demands, their values increased faster than the rate of inflation.

Common stocks, which had responded favorably to the modest inflation of the 1950s and 1960s, were thought by many to be capable of protecting investors against inflation. However, common stocks did poorly during the 1970s—a period of rising inflation, falling productivity, increased foreign competition, and rising energy costs. The Dow-Jones average is a compilation of the stock values drawn from thirty of the largest companies in America. These companies represent a cross section of American business. The Dow-Jones average had reached 1000 by the mid-1960s but remained in the 600 to 1000 range until the autumn of 1982.

Although common stocks performed poorly, the real losers were those who owned long-term bonds that paid fixed, low rates of interest. As the value of these bonds declined, so did the purchasing power of the interest and principal of payments received by the bondholders.

Those who held their money in bank accounts and money market funds saw the purchasing power of their dollars decrease as a result of the inflation. This decrease was offset to some degree, however, by high interest rates paid on such accounts. Great demand for cash during this period caused abnormally high interest rates, with 15 percent or more per annum typical on the safest of investments.

By 1980 economists were projecting continued inflation to be the dominant economic factor in the coming decade. Government deficits, considered by many to be the single most important cause of inflation, were projected to remain exceedingly high during the entire decade.

Although deficits remained high through 1985 and are projected to continue so during the second half of the decade, inflation began to decline soon after the election of President Reagan in 1980. This decline was contrary to most investor expectations. In the course of two years, inflation was reduced to an annual rate of less than 5 percent. During this two-year period, the market value of gold, silver, and other hard assets dropped precipitously from their 1980 highs. In the summer of 1982, both the stock and bond markets rallied dramatically. This was due primarily to the drop in the rate of inflation and an easing of interest rates.

Those who acquired long-term treasury bonds when interest rates were double-digit (ranging from 10 percent to 15 percent) had indeed made a wise investment. For the first time in years, the market favored those who acquired bonds that could be held for a long period of time with fixed and guaranteed returns.

Those investors in the 1950s and 1960s who were conscious of the depression of the 1930s and its problems put a high priority on safety of principal and invested in high-quality bonds and bank accounts that were guaranteed by the federal government. They unwittingly assumed the greatest risk of all, the risk that has plagued the economies of nations for centuries: inflation. Those investors who bought gold in 1980, justifiably anticipating continued hyperinflation, paid a heavy price for their lessons in economics and investing as they watched the value of gold and other hard assets decline by more than 50 percent in two years.

In each case the quality of the investment was very high. Thus, there was little risk in the investment itself—that is, little investment risk—but such investments suffered from market risk changes in the economy that adversely affected the value of bonds and gold.

Apart from the risks inherent in the investment and in the market, you assume an additional risk when you make an investment because a promoter expresses a belief that it holds the potential for great reward. This kind of risk, with its get-rich-quick promise, is simply foolish and unacceptable to an experienced investor. It is foolish because it is based on a promoter's promise and an investor's ignorance. Such promoters often thrive in strong markets when virtually every investment in a given category looks good. During these times, investors are often talked into low-quality, high-return investments that lose their value at the first downturn in that particular market.

Successful investors, like successful businesspeople, acquire the facts and realistically evaluate the potential for both success and failure. Lee Iacocca, often considered a guy who shoots from the hip, referred to this in his recent best-selling autobiography, *Iacocca*. He stated that his management style is conservative, saying, "Whenever I've taken risks, it's been after satisfying myself that the research and the market study supported my instincts. I may act on my intuition—but only if my hunches are supported by the facts."

MINIMIZING RISKS

Regardless of how conservative we choose to be, we can never be guaranteed that any investment will retain its value in future years. Changes in the economy are difficult if not impossible to anticipate. You must understand and accept that these unforeseen events may occur and will directly affect your investments.

In attempting to minimize risk, some investors choose to invest in one asset or in one category of assets, such as real property, stocks, or bonds. These investors adopt a theory of putting their eggs in one basket and never taking their eyes off the basket. Consequently they maintain close control over their investments and are extremely knowledgeable about the area in which they are investing.

Most investors adopt a balanced approach to investment and market risk by seeking both quality and diversification. They own a variety of investments. For example, they own real property (their homes and other investments in real property), along with more liquid assets such as stocks, bonds, and money market funds. They diversify stock holdings by investing in a reasonable number of corporations representing the basic industries and businesses of America. Their bond purchases are diversified among U.S.-government, utility-company, corporate, and tax-free bonds of the highest quality. In so doing they attempt to balance and minimize the impact of changes on their overall investments.

THE IMPORTANCE OF DEFINING INVESTMENT OBJECTIVES

In addition to understanding the risks inherent in any investment, you must also define your objectives so that you can choose those particular investments that are consistent with your goals. There is much confusion in defining investment objectives. Promoters often ask you to define your investment objectives by answering a series of questions: Do you want an investment that will reduce your income taxes? Do you want an investment that will protect you against inflation? Do you want an investment that has been owned by virtually every successful investor during the past twenty-five years?

The answers are always predictable: "yes." Unfortunately, the questions have nothing to do with forming valid investment objectives. Their sole purpose is to promote an investment and gain your confidence by having you indulge in nothing more than wishful thinking. The promoter's purpose in having you adopt objectives of this kind is no different than his or her purpose in having you think of yourself as an aggressive risk taker—to entice you to purchase a particular investment or investment product.

Investment objectives are always personal and unique to each individual. Your choice of investments will depend on your age, your other assets, your income, your income potential, your concerns about security, your concerns about inflation, your fears of a depression, your need for a guaranteed income, the amount of time you are willing to devote to managing your investments, and numerous other personal considerations.

It is these concerns, hopes, and desires that should determine your particular investments. You must therefore learn what to expect from each investment—its advantages, its disadvantages, and how it will respond in times of inflation, recession, or depression. Acquiring such understanding of what to expect from a particular investment is really not difficult. It becomes difficult when we invest based on predictions of the future course of the economy and when we invest in areas in which we have absolutely no knowledge and therefore no business investing our money. Good investing is common sense. You can do it as well as anyone, provided you keep in mind the "great secret" and avoid being a bad investor—taking foolish risks.

You take control by understanding the potential risks and rewards of the various categories of investments and by choosing those investments in each category that are consistent with your objectives. If you don't take control, the risk you assume is a session on the park bench. It's that simple.

CHAPTER 3

Playing the Interest Game

*It is better to have a permanent income
than to be fascinating.*

Oscar Wilde

There are only two ways to invest your money. You can loan it and play the interest game, or you can purchase an asset or an interest in an asset and take an ownership (an equity) position. In this chapter, we will take a look at the interest game.

When you deposit your money in a bank account, loan it to a friend, or buy a government or corporate bond, you are playing the interest game. And you are in demand. The federal and state governments, banks, insurance companies, and numerous other institutions and individuals want to borrow your money.

What kind of investment are you looking for when you play this game? You want an investment that will pay you the highest annual rate of interest on your money and will at the same time guarantee the safe return of your principal. You also want to know: (1) How available is your money if you want it back? (2) What is the inflation risk? (3) Are there any tax advantages?

THE RELATIONSHIP BETWEEN
INTEREST AND SECURITY

Government and Corporate Bonds

When you loan your money to the United States government, you have made the securest loan possible. You make this loan when you purchase a treasury bill, a treasury note, or a treasury bond. A treasury bill is a loan of your money to the U.S. government for less than a year; a treasury note is a loan of your money for one to ten years; and a treasury bond is a loan of your money for ten to forty years. The repayment of these loans and the interest is a direct obligation of the U.S. government and is guaranteed by its full faith and credit.

Because a direct loan to the U.S. government provides the greatest protection of your principal, it will pay the lowest rate of interest. Interest rates on all other types of loans, including bonds issued by agencies of the federal government, will be higher than those paid by the federal government on its direct obligations.

More than a hundred federal government agencies issue bonds. Although these bonds are not direct obligations of the federal government, most of them are guaranteed by it and are therefore considered very secure. Bonds issued by these federal agencies will generally pay from 0.5 percent to 1 percent more in interest than a comparable U.S. Treasury obligation.

Corporations and utility companies also borrow your money and issue bonds. These bonds are rated according to their safety. A rating of their safety is nothing more than a projection of the borrower's ability to make the payments of interest and principal when due. Based on the borrower's financial strength or weakness at any given time, the projection is always subject to change. For example, a company's bonds might be downgraded if it runs into financial difficulties.

A number of firms rate these bonds on the basis of their quality. The two best-known rating firms are Standard & Poor's and Moody's. They rate bonds as "Prime" (Triple A), "Excellent" (Double A), and "Good" (Single A). Bonds with a rating of Triple B or lower are those of companies whose financial situations suggest that they may have trouble paying your interest and principal when due. The possibility that they will fail to make these payments is far greater when the economy is depressed. The highest-rated corporate and utility bonds will pay from 1 to 2 percentage points more in interest than a U.S. Treasury obligation will pay (or "will yield") for the same period of time.

Because corporations and utility companies have fewer problems in paying their obligations during times of prosperity, a bond rating becomes more significant the longer you intend to hold the bond. The longer the period, the greater the likelihood that the economy will suffer a recession or even depression, during which a corporation may have difficulty meeting its obligations.

But you should not confuse even the highest ratings with guarantees. A company's ability to continue to pay the interest on your debt and to repay the principal can change. The best (or worst) example of this situation appears in the case of the bonds issued by the state of Washington Public Power Supply System (WPPSS) in the 1970s. At the time these bonds were issued, they were given the highest rating possible. They were sold in order to finance the construction of two nuclear power plants. Years later the utility company announced that it could not meet its obligations and thus precipitated the largest default in municipal bond history. In an attempt to recover their investments, the holders of WPPSS bonds became plaintiffs in one of the largest lawsuits ever filed against a state. These investors find little humor in Mark Twain's statement, "I don't care about a return on my investment; I only care about a return of my investment."

In order to provide maximum security of your principal, it is always wise to diversify your loan investments by purchasing high-quality bonds from various borrowers. The deterioration in the value of the WPPSS bonds clearly proved that "ratings" should never be confused with "guarantees."

Banks, Savings and Loans, and Money Markets

Banks and savings and loan associations have money accounts that vary in the interest rate they pay and the period for which your money is committed. Some of these are demand accounts—meaning that you may withdraw your cash at any time. Others will yield a fixed rate of interest for a given period of time (three months, one year, or even longer). You will generally be paid a higher rate of interest for agreeing to leave your money in these accounts for a longer period. You can withdraw your principal at any time, but you will lose the higher interest as a penalty for the early withdrawal.

So-called money market funds are established and maintained by banks, savings and loans, and brokerage firms and other investment institutions. These funds reinvest your money in short-term treasury bills and other well-secured short-term loan instruments. The interest they receive is passed on to you, the original investor. Although money market funds are not guaranteed by the federal government, many of them reinvest your money in bills, notes, bonds, and bank accounts that are. The quality of these funds and the security of your investment will vary according to the type of note or bond the fund purchases with your money.

The relationship between the rate of interest investors receive and the security of their principal was recently dramatized to more than twelve thousand disgruntled depositors of the Western Community Money Center, a California thrift institution that recently filed for bankruptcy. Although each Money Center account was insured for up to $50,000 by a California state agency, the depositors discovered that they might have to wait as long as ten years to receive their money because they cannot be paid in full until after all the assets of the thrift institution have been liquidated. Referring to the frustrations of these investors, Franklin Thom, the California state commissioner of corporations, said, "We all have a lot of alternatives in where to place our money. There is a ratio between risk and reward. Thrifts offer a higher and better rate of return for taking a greater degree of risk."

This principle was demonstrated in a 1985 segment of "60 Minutes." The segment dealt with a nonbank financial institution in Nebraska that paid a higher rate of interest than competing banks. When this institution filed for bankruptcy in late 1983, the state agency guaranteeing its deposits did not have nearly enough money to back up its guarantees. With much anxiety and at great expense, the depositors attempted to require the state of Nebraska to make up for their losses.

A number of financial institutions that deal in money market funds appear to be banks or savings and loan associations but are not. Many of them are insured by state agencies, but they do not carry the same kind of federal guarantee that banks and savings and loan associations do.

Promissory Notes Secured by Real Property

The highest rate of interest on money you loan is often paid on promissory notes secured by mortgages or deeds of trust on real property.

Many individuals acquire these notes in order to sell their homes. In a typical case, a buyer cannot finance the purchase of a home because of high interest rates. So the seller, instead of receiving cash from the buyer, takes back the buyer's interest-bearing promissory note for all or part of the purchase price. The buyer's payments are secured by a deed of trust on the real property he or she has just purchased.

Owners of real property who want to borrow money often secure their loans by giving the lender a note, the payment of which is secured by the borrower's real property. There are even companies that act as intermediaries between lenders and borrowers. These companies have as clients private investors who are willing to loan their money on these notes secured by deeds of trust.

Unless you are a trader in this kind of loan, are familiar with the real property pledged as security, know its value, and are reliably informed about the financial responsibility of the individual borrowing the money, you are often assuming a very great risk in exchange for the additional interest that you will receive on this kind of loan as compared to other high-quality notes and bonds available in the marketplace.

Notes secured by deeds of trust will often pay 4 to 5 percent more in interest than a lender can receive on comparable U.S. Treasury obligations. But if the borrower defaults on the loan, you may be required to take title to the real property in lieu of a return of your principal and payments of the interest you have earned. If other investors have loaned money on the security of the same property (this occurs whenever your deed of trust or mortgage is not a first, but rather a second or third), you may even be required to assume these obligations in order to protect your principal. If you find it necessary to foreclose on your security, you will often encounter delays and costs that you did not anticipate.

The Woodson Company, a mortgage lending and investment company in San Rafael, California, was reported in 1985 to have sold more than $60 million in such notes secured by deeds of trust on real property. The company held many of these loans for the investors. According to a publication list, twenty-two hundred investors had made loans ranging from $15,000 to $115,000. These investors were stunned upon receiving notification that the Woodson Company had filed for bankruptcy. They were also told that all interest payments on their investments would halt until a plan for reorganization had been approved by the bankruptcy court. Many of these investors were elderly and had placed virtually all their money in these loans in order to receive a little extra interest.

Thus, whenever you are offered a rate of interest greater than that you could receive on treasury bonds, high-quality utility bonds, or federally secured bank accounts, you can be sure of one thing: you are assuming a greater risk in the return of your principal and in the assurance that interest will be paid as promised.

UNDERSTANDING LIQUIDITY AND MARKETABILITY

In addition to the amount of interest you receive and the security of your principal, *liquidity* is an important consideration. Put simply, liquidity means that if you want your money back, you can receive it immediately or in a relatively short time.

Bank accounts, money market funds, and treasury bills are all highly liquid; your money is available on demand. When you purchase bonds and notes that are not due for years, the only way you can receive your principal immediately is to sell the obligation. If there are many available buyers and the obligation is easily sold, it is said to be *marketable;* it can readily be turned into cash.

U.S. Treasury obligations, government-agency bonds guaranteed by the federal government, and high-quality corporate and utility bonds are easily sold on an established market.

Bonds that are not of the highest quality, including many tax-free bonds, are not readily marketable. In many cases bonds of this kind can only be sold if the seller is willing to take a substantial loss. Promissory notes secured by deeds of trust on real property can also be difficult if not impossible to liquidate because they are sold in a market with a limited number of buyers.

The fact that a bond is marketable, however, does not mean you will necessarily get all your money back. When a bond is sold before its due date, you may receive more dollars than you paid for it or fewer dollars than you paid for it, depending on changes in the interest rates after you purchased your bond. If interest rates have risen since you purchased your bond, its market value will have gone down, and you will receive fewer dollars than you invested. If interest rates have dropped since you purchased your bond, its market value will have increased, and you will receive more dollars than you invested.

For example, assume you acquired a utility-company bond that pays 10 percent per annum for ten years. One year later you decide you want to sell. At that time, the interest rate on a comparable bond of the same quality and term is 11 percent per annum. Any buyer would prefer to have a bond paying 11 percent per annum rather than your bond paying 10 percent per annum, all other considerations being equal. Therefore, in order to sell your bond, you must reduce its price from what you paid so that a buyer will receive the going rate of 11 percent per annum on the investment. This means that a $10,000 bond that pays $1,000 per annum interest can sell for $9,090 and thus will pay the new buyer 11 percent per annum because he or she receives $1,000 per annum on an investment of $9,090.

Now assume that after you acquire your bond, the same quality bond is paying only 9 percent per annum. Thus your bond paying 10 percent per annum is more valuable and will sell at an increased price (more than you paid for it) because a buyer demands only a 9 percent per annum return. Your $10,000 bond paying $1,000 per annum will now sell for $11,111, which represents a 9 percent return on the new buyer's investment.

Thus, the value of your bond will adjust either up or down as the interest rates move up or down, but always in the opposite direction. The values decrease when the rates go up and increase when the rates go down.

Obviously, the trick is to buy bonds when interest rates are at their peak. When the rates fall, the value of your bond will increase. When interest rates rise dramatically as they did in the late 1970s and early 1980s (making these years a good time to buy), you will read that the bond market is *depressed*. The statement that the market is depressed applies to bond-holders who had previously purchased bonds that have a lower interest rate. When the market is depressed is often the best time to buy bonds because this means that the current market interest rates are higher than they were. That's when you want to buy bonds—when the market is depressed— because interest rates are at their peak. Conversely, you have to be more careful when interest rates have dropped and the value of bonds has appreciated. If you buy bonds at that point, you are vulnerable to the interest rates turning around and increasing and thus reducing the market value of your bonds paying the lower rates.

THE INFLATION RISK

An important factor to be considered in every loan invest-ment, whether short-, medium-, or long-term, is the risk of inflation, or what might be called the *purchasing power risk*.

When you invest your money in bank accounts and other loan investments, you are vulnerable to the risk of inflation. During times of inflation, the cost of goods and services rises. The same number of dollars that would have purchased a basket of food, a home, or a new car in 1970 was not sufficient to buy the same amount of food or that same quality home or car ten years later. When this occurs, your dollars have lost a portion of their purchasing power. The extent of that loss will depend on the rate of inflation. As many retired individuals have discovered during the past fifteen years, inflation can turn what was a very secure, comfortable retirement into one that threatens a reduced standard of living.

Although all loan investments are adversely affected by inflation, some are affected less than others. Money invested in bank accounts, savings and loan accounts, and money market funds does lose its purchasing power during times of inflation. However, because these moneys are not committed for long periods of time, and can be withdrawn on demand or on relatively short notice, the rates of interest on these investments will adjust to reflect the higher interest rates usually brought about by inflation. For example, from 1979 into 1982, the rates on certificates of deposit and money market accounts ranged from 15 to 17 percent per annum. Even though the purchasing power of the dollars in these accounts declined because of inflation, the depositors had a much easier time dealing with higher prices because of the greater amount of interest they were receiving on their deposits.

However, if you loan your money for a longer period of time, which is what you do when you purchase a bond due in ten or twenty years, the market value of your investment is affected by inflation in two ways. First, you are locked into a fixed rate of interest, which means that you are not able to take advantage of the higher rates of interest in the market-place. Second, the purchasing power of the interest and principal is further reduced. The longer the term of your bond at a rate of interest lower than the market rate, the greater your loss will be if it is necessary for you to sell.

It is for these reasons that many investors who play the interest game diversify their loan investments among short-, medium-, and long-term. They balance these loans according to the going rates of interest when they invest. They favor long-term loan investments when interest rates are high and favor short-term and medium-term loan investments when interest rates are low and thus vulnerable to a subsequent rise.

At any given time, long-term bonds generally pay several percentage points more in interest than short-term loan investments. This is necessary because of the inflation risk that the purchaser of a long-term bond is assuming. It is this additional interest that entices investors to buy long-term bonds.

There are also potential rewards in acquiring long-term bonds. First, you may lock in a rate of interest that is much higher than the current market rate. If interest rates remain constant or go down, you will usually receive several percentage points more in interest for a long-term bond than if you had invested in current obligations such as bank accounts and money market funds. Second, if you sell when interest rates are down, you will get more than you paid.

TAX CONSIDERATIONS

When you play the interest game, you must consider how federal and state governments will tax the interest on your investments. States, counties, cities, school districts, universities, and numerous other government agencies and political subdivisions can issue bonds that pay interest that is not included in your income for federal income tax purposes. These are commonly called *tax-free* or *municipal (muni)* bonds.

Municipal bonds, like corporate and utility bonds, are rated by Moody's and Standard & Poor's. These ratings are significant with regard to the protection of your principal and the marketability of the bonds. Municipal bonds that are not rated or are given lower ratings may be difficult to sell on the open market. Often a seller must be willing to take a substantial loss in order to find a buyer.

Even though the interest paid on a municipal bond is exempt from federal income tax, it may or may not be exempt from state income tax. In California, for example, the interest on a tax-free bond issued by another state is, for California residents, subject to California state income tax. Interest received by California residents on bonds issued by the state of California or other California state agencies is not subject to either federal or California income tax.

Interest on federal obligations, such as U.S. Treasury obligations and obligations issued by various federal agencies, is not subject to state income tax. Thus, even though the interest you receive on federal bonds is generally subject to federal income tax, this interest escapes state income taxation. Additionally, a tax-free bond, like any bond for a fixed period, can increase or decrease in value, depending on the future direction of interest rates.

Some investors in high tax brackets who want to defer (not avoid) taxes on their income have been attracted to what is called a *single premium deferred annuity*. This annuity is in effect a savings account held by an insurance company. As such, it is a loan by you to the insurance company. An annuity of this type is not guaranteed by the federal government. If you invest in one, your principal is secured by the assets of the life insurance company. You should therefore be careful to purchase it from a company that has the highest financial rating. (A. M. Best rates insurance companies according to their financial strength in *Best's.*)

Such an annuity gives you the advantage of avoiding taxation on the accumulated interest until you withdraw it. Although you can withdraw your money at any time, your cash is committed to the insurance company for an agreed number of years. If you withdraw it earlier, you will pay a penalty. The penalty would be in addition to your tax liability on the accumulated interest.

BEWARE OF THE CALL

For bond buyers who feel that current interest rates are high and will probably decline or that interest rates will not change much in the foreseeable future and who therefore want the higher rates offered by long-term bonds, it is important to know whether the bond being considered contains a *call* provision. A call provision allows the borrower—the corporation, the utility company, the municipality—to pay off the bond prior to its due date, usually with a small *bonus,* or premium. Assume, for example, that you buy a corporate bond in the face amount of $10,000 that pays 12 percent interest per annum and is due in twenty-five years. The corporation is obligated to pay the bondholder $1,200 a year interest each and every year for twenty-five years and to repay the principal amount of $10,000 at the end of the twenty-five-year period.

If the bond contains a provision that states the corporation can redeem it in ten years by paying a premium of 2 percent over the face amount of the bond, then you have purchased a bond with a call provision. This means that the corporation can terminate its obligation before the twenty-five years are up if it elects to pay you the $10,000 face amount of the bond plus an additional $200 as a premium on the call date. Only the corporation can terminate the obligation early. You do not have the same option. If the corporation does not elect to pay you off (which it will not do if interest rates are higher), then you are locked into receiving lower interest payments for the full twenty-five-year term of the bond.

If interest rates are lower than 12 percent on the call date, the corporation will borrow money at the lower rates (by issuing more bonds) and exercise its call rights. You will receive a premium, but that is small comfort if you have to go back into the marketplace and purchase a bond of comparable quality and duration but receive a lower rate of interest. In short, a call provision is, for the investor, simply a "heads I (the investor) lose, tails they (the corporation) win" proposition.

When you acquire a long-term bond, you assume the risk that interest rates might rise and that the market value of your bond will consequently decrease. Furthermore, you assume the risk that continued inflation will have eroded the purchasing power of dollars paid back to you at some time in the future. When you purchase a long-term bond with the intention of holding it, there is a potential reward if interest rates decline. If that occurs, you will have locked in a much higher rate of interest than would be available to you in the future. Should interest rates decline, and should the economy go into a recession or depression, your long-term bonds at the higher interest rates will indeed be a wise investment.

If you have invested in a corporate bond that requires the borrower to pay you 13 percent per annum for twenty-five years, and if the current interest rate on a bond of comparable quality and duration is 8 percent per annum, you can be sure that the borrower (the corporation) will be delighted to redeem your bond at its face amount and pay you the premium on the call date, which will save it a substantial amount of interest in the future and deprive you of that same interest.

Surprisingly, call provisions do not usually appear in treasury bonds, which are bonds of the highest quality. A treasury bond purchased for twenty or thirty years will lock in its rate of interest for the full duration of the bond.

Investors will often buy bonds issued by government agencies, rather than those that are the direct obligations of the government itself, because of the slightly higher rate of interest received on bonds issued by these agencies. The most popular bonds of this kind are issued by the Government National Mortgage Association (*Ginnie Maes*), the Federal National Mortgage Association (*Fannie Maes*), and the Federal Home Loan Mortgage Corporation (*Freddie Macs*). All three of these agencies issue bonds offering higher yields than U.S. Treasury obligations and are backed by mortgages. Ginnie Mae bonds are the most secure in this category because the issuing agency holds FHA and VA mortgages guaranteed by the federal government. The Fannie Maes and Freddie Macs hold conventional mortgages, which are not guaranteed by the federal government. However, these bonds are considered to have minimal credit risk.

The bonds issued by all three of these agencies pay interest and principal monthly. Because they pay off the principal, they are not appropriate investments for investors who intend to lock in a particular rate of interest for a given period of time. They are not, for example, the same as buying a twenty-year treasury bond, which will pay interest (but not principal) during the twenty-year period.

The Ginnie Maes, Fannie Maes, and Freddie Macs may be excellent investments for someone who wants to be paid both interest and principal monthly and who wants to receive the highest return on a secure investment during the period of time that the principal is being repaid. When interest rates drop, as they did in 1985 and the first part of 1986, the Ginnie Maes, Fannie Maes, and Freddie Macs will be paid off long before their due dates because these bonds are backed by mortgages. When interest rates fall, homeowners refinance at the lower rates of interest and thus pay off the existing mortgages early. Unfortunately, this is exactly when investors do not want their principal repaid, preferring to continue to receive the higher rate of interest. Upon receiving their principal, those who reinvest will receive the current lower rates of interest.

Those who play the interest game have come to accept that the future direction of interest rates is virtually impossible to predict. This was particularly true during the period between 1975 and 1985, when the interest "gurus" were grabbing the headlines and later explaining why their predictions weren't fulfilled.

Loan investments provide an important balance in most investment planning. This is particularly true when they are a part of a retirement plan (such as a Keogh plan or IRA account) with the tax deferral benefits. Chapter 6 compares the growth of interest investments in retirement plans to some of the more traditional growth-type investments. The results can be surprising.

CHAPTER 4

The Equity Investor

*The best fertilizer
is the owner's footprint.*
Robert H. Walter

Unlike those who play the interest game and plan on a return of their principal, equity investors risk their capital to acquire a "piece of the action." Their principal is always at risk. Although every investment, including a loan investment, can increase or decrease in value, the primary objective of equity investors is appreciation. There are two basic types of equity investors: *active* and *passive.*

ACTIVE INVESTORS

Equity investors who control the investment are active investors. The sole proprietor of a small business, the owner of commercial real property, the real estate developer, and the stock and bond trader on the floor of the New York Stock Exchange are all examples of active investors. Active investors are able to control their investments after their money is committed.

Active investors succeed or fail for a variety of reasons. Knowledge, effort, ability to adapt to changes in the economy, and on occasion, good or bad fortune are all factors. Although the failure rate among active investors is high, most rags to riches stories are about active investors. Active investors range from individual entrepreneurs to multinational corporate conglomerates—from the most conservative to the greatest of risk takers. They vary in their experiences and skills. They can be as different as Mozart and the young man in his early twenties who approached him and asked how he should prepare himself to write symphonies. Mozart told him that, considering his young age, he should begin by writing ballads. "But," he said, "you were writing symphonies at the age of ten." "Yes," replied Mozart, "but I wasn't asking how." Like those who write symphonies, active investors either know how, learn how, or fail. The result is theirs to determine.

PASSIVE INVESTORS

Unlike active investors, passive investors are not in a position to make decisions that affect the survival or failure of their investments. Once their money is committed, their control over the investment is limited. The owner of common stocks bought and sold on the New York Stock Exchange, the limited partner in a limited partnership, and the purchaser of an interest in a mutual fund are all examples of passive investors.

Passive investors have only one opportunity to evaluate each investment and its risks—before they commit their money. So they are far more limited in their investment choices than are active investors. The risk assumed by passive investors is entirely different than that assumed by active investors. It is not necessarily greater; it is just different. It requires passive investors to take a more conservative approach to investing.

Both active and passive investors need to know and understand their investments and the general market conditions when they make their initial investments. But even if passive investors are knowledgeable about the market in which they are about to invest (and this varies greatly among passive investors, with many being totally ignorant), it is often difficult if not impossible for them to adequately assess the investment risk involved. If they later discover that their risk is greater than they first assumed, their lack of control over their investments renders them incapable of doing anything about it.

Each day in the financial pages of newspapers and magazines you'll find stories of passive investors who lost their money because of fraud, misrepresentation, or the high-risk nature of the investment. These stories are not limited to the financially naive, but include individuals and institutions that are experienced in financial matters. For example, the Bank of America recently acted as trustee for investors who bought notes secured by real property that turned out to be worth far less than the amount the investors paid. Although the bank acted as trustee and guaranteed to the investors that these notes were sound, the facts showed that the bank knew virtu ally nothing about their value and had not conducted any investigation. The bank was required to acknowledge approximately $100,000,000 liability to the investors. Darrell Johnson, a vice-president of the bank, was quoted as having said, "We had never done this kind of business before, and were never supposed to have done it."

An article in the April 1985 issue of *Money* is about well-known and successful businessmen who made investments for the wrong reasons. These investors included Lee Iacocca, president of Chrysler, Norman Lear, TV producer, and Arthur Laffer, architect of the supply-side economic doctrine. Harry Cunningham, retired chairman and chief executive of K-Mart, and several of his friends who were members of Detroit's prestigious Bloomfield Hills Country Club invested in Weaver

Exploration, a company that sponsored oil and gas shelters. When they discovered that they would lose most of their capital and face back taxes as well, Mr. Cunningham admitted, "We knew nothing about the oil business." These businessmen made investments based not on their experience and knowledge in the area, but on what they heard and were told. And each lost hundreds of thousands of dollars.

When successful people make poor investments, they do so because they have come to believe either in their own infallibility or that of someone they greatly respect. As a passive investor, you should never make any investment based solely on someone else's recommendation, regardless of how successful that person is, particularly when that person also has a passive role in the investment.

Passive investors who want to build an estate must be realistic in their investment expectations by making sure they receive *value* at the time they make each investment. How do they do this? They do this by investing in established markets to which they have direct access and by selecting investments in those markets that are consistent with their investment objectives.

Passive investors have a variety of investment choices that they can make in established markets. In addition to the loan investments discussed in Chapter 3, here are some of the more common investment markets available to the passive investor and some factors to be considered when making the investment.

Gold, Silver, and Other Hard Assets

Passive investors can purchase gold, silver, diamonds and other precious gems, old coins, stamps, works of art, and antiques. These items are purchased for appreciation and as a hedge against inflation.

You buy gold and silver by purchasing coins made of these metals through established brokerage firms and other reputable dealers, who may charge large commissions if they are dealing in small quantities. Because gold and silver are traded daily, their values are readily established. Two disadvantages are that such investments provide no yields (dividends or interest) and can be difficult and expensive to store.

Diamonds and other precious gems, old coins, stamps, works of art, and antiques are sold in more limited and specialized markets. Those who acquire these assets as investments are often very knowledgeable (active investors) or are brokers who acquire these investments on behalf of their wealthy clients. These kinds of assets often require experts to distinguish special differences among them that affect their value. If you acquire one of these assets from a promoter and are not entirely knowledgeable, it is probable that you would be getting less than value and the likelihood of its appreciation would be relatively remote.

If you desire to sell gold and silver, they are readily salable, as long as the market is "hot." Otherwise you will probably sell at substantial discounts (25 percent or more). The other categories of hard assets are difficult to liquidate because of the limited market. Furthermore, you will often be required to bear a substantial discount, particularly in a depressed market, in order to cash out your investment.

Of course, passive investors may purchase stock in the companies that own, invest in, and control these assets. The shares of these companies generally increase or decrease in value with the consumer demand for the assets.

Real Estate

Real estate has probably produced more millionaires in this country than any other investment. From 1945 through 1980, real estate has provided investors with excellent protection from inflation, substantial appreciation, and a solid income base. In addition to appreciation in value, commercial and rental properties provide a tax advantage to the investor in the form of depreciation that is deducted against current income. Property taxes and interest payments on any loans necessary to acquire or improve the property are also deductible.

However, the vast majority of successful investors in real estate are active. They are familiar with the market, and they retain control over their investment once it is made. Buying a home, for example, has been the best investment many people have made during the past twenty years.

There are a number of excellent books on how to be a successful investor in real estate. Howard G. Allen's best-selling book *Creating Wealth* is one of them. However, the approaches and techniques require that you be actively involved and willing to spend a great amount of time and effort in acquiring, maintaining, and selling these properties. To be a successful investor in real estate and create an estate, you must be willing to make sacrifices. Because real property is often acquired with borrowed funds, the interest payments, property taxes, insurance, and other costs will often equal or exceed the income derived from the property. Its acquisition and maintenance require time and money that many will prefer to spend on more immediate pleasures.

Real estate is an investment acquired for the long term. It should never be acquired with the idea of a quick profit, and although there is always a market for real estate, it is not considered liquid (readily salable for cash). However, because of the long-term inflation potential of our economy due to the large government deficits, acquiring a home and other commercial properties provides a basis for investment diversification that cannot be obtained by only investing in stocks, bonds, and bank accounts.

The Stock Market

The stock market provides passive investors with opportunities to invest in companies that are engaged in every business activity in the world. They can diversify among a variety of investments. Some stocks pay high dividends, some stocks pay little or no dividends but are purchased primarily for appreciation, and many stocks of long-established blue chip companies pay reasonable dividends with a hope that they will grow with the economy.

There are approximately nineteen hundred companies whose shares of stock are traded on the New York Stock Exchange. When you read that the stock market is up or the stock market is down, it is usually because of changes in either the Standard & Poor's Index or the Dow-Jones Index. The Standard & Poor's Index reflects the increases and decreases of five hundred of the stocks listed on the New York Stock Exchange; the Dow-Jones Index reflects the increases and decreases of thirty of the largest companies whose stocks are actively traded on the New York exchange.

The companies that form a part of the Dow-Jones and Standard & Poor's compilations and every other company listed on the New York Stock Exchange are analyzed daily by thousands of individuals. These analysts provide their opinions to pension funds, mutual funds, brokerage firms, and millions of individual investors who buy and sell on these recommendations.

The Infinite Wisdom Theory

Because of the large number of individuals analyzing the stock of each company on the New York Stock Exchange, their collective conclusions (often conflicting) are immediately reflected in the price of that stock. If more people want to purchase shares of a stock than want to sell them, the price per share will increase to reflect this demand. And if those desiring to sell outnumber those desiring to buy, the price will drop. Thus at any given moment the price of any given stock sold on the New York Stock Exchange reflects all the known considerations and expectations, including anticipated changes that may occur in the market, the industry, or the economy. All these factors will directly bear on the price of these shares.

So it is said that the stock market has *infinite wisdom.* And this wisdom is reflected in the current value of these shares. By subscribing to the infinite wisdom theory of the stock market, your underlying philosophy is to acquire stocks that will produce a fair and stable rate of return through both dividends and appreciation. It requires you to focus on the value you are acquiring and your long-term investment objectives rather than on the expectation of immediate gain.

P-E Ratios

Buying stocks of companies that are selling at a low *price-earnings ratio* and that otherwise meet your criteria and objectives is good assurance that you are getting value at the time the stocks are acquired. For example, if the stock of a company is selling at $10 a share and the annual earnings of that company are $1 for each share of stock outstanding, then the price of each share in relation to company earnings is a ratio of 10 to 1. If the stock is selling at $20 a share, then for each share outstanding its price-earnings ratio is 20 to 1. Stocks that sell at a high price-earnings ratio do so because investors anticipate future economic expansion for the company, increased company earnings, followed by increased value in the stock. This anticipation is in turn reflected both in the value of the stock and the high price-earnings ratio. Likewise, stocks that are selling at a low price-earnings ratio are doing so because of the market, the industry, or because that particular company's potential for increased earnings is not recognized.

Since 1935, the average price-earnings ratio of stocks that make up the Dow-Jones Industrial Average has ranged from a high of 26 to 1 for stocks of quality companies to a low of 6 to 1. Thus, many analysts consider that a price-earnings ratio in the range of 10 to 1 or lower is a very favorable indicator of value, particularly for strong companies that are the leaders in their industries.

Quick-Profit Strategies

Wall Street investment analysts often promote the purchase of so-called undervalued stocks. They imply that these stocks are virtually guaranteed to increase to their true values, and that this increase in value will occur within a relatively short period of time.

Under the infinite wisdom theory of the stock market, there are no undervalued shares. Investors who attempt to buy the so-called undervalued stocks for a quick profit are engaging in high-risk investing. Those who adopt this approach and make impulsive forays into the market in the hope of capitalizing on such opportunities soon become disheartened. They often withdraw from the market, failing to understand the futility of their approach and the unnecessary risk they assumed.

Investor or Trader

A well-known financial writer told the story of a friend who turned $400 into $18,000 in four months by trading stock options, an extremely high-risk investment. She said, however, that within six months he had lost the $18,000 and then some (including a loan from her). She asked, "Do you want to have a little fun playing the market and probably lose some money (trading), or go the boring, effortful way and maybe make a little money (investing)?" She suggested that when the question is put that way, everyone chooses to be an investor. However, she said, "In real life we tend to be traders while identifying ourselves as investors."

Professional traders in common stocks, bonds, and options on the floor of the New York Stock Exchange are *active investors.* They have immediate access to the market, they understand its volatility, and they make their living by trading—not by advising people like you and me how to do it. If you want to be a trader in the stock market, then be one. But don't confuse being an investor with being a trader.

A Prudent Approach

As a passive investor, how do you develop a strategy to select quality stocks consistent with your own investment philosophy? You become knowledgeable about the stocks that are available to you. You buy stocks of financially secure companies whose market prices are reasonable with their current earnings and expectations. You understand how various changes in the economy might affect the value of these shares either favorably or unfavorably. You listen to the experts, and you listen to the approaches taken by the experts.

Florence Fearington, a guest on the popular "Wall Street Week" television program, was introduced as one who has an enviable record for picking stocks. She described her investment philosophy as follows: "I look for entrenched companies, very strong companies, soundly financed and selling at a very low price-earnings ratio in the marketplace." She emphasized that her orientation was long-term and that she did not pay attention to either rises or falls in the market; nor was she interested in the latest rumor from the wire room.

You adopt the Fearington approach by acquiring and holding shares of companies that are leaders in their particular industries—stocks of companies that pay dividends and hold the promise of sharing in the long-term economic growth of America. There are numerous reports designed to provide investors with complete information on the history and current status of all the companies listed on the New York Stock Exchange. The stock guide published by Standard & Poor's is considered to be among the best and most informative.

Full-service brokerage firms also provide their clients with much useful information on the stocks of companies that comprise the Dow-Jones and Standard & Poor's indexes. Their reports state the current price of the stock, the price range in which it has been trading during the prior twelve months, its current dividends and dividend history, the estimated earnings of the company for the coming year, the current price of the stock in relation to its current earnings, and the current price of the stock in relation to its current dividends.

As a passive investor, you purchase stocks in good-quality companies because they provide you the best opportunity to share in America's economic prosperity. You also acquire an interest in companies that can best survive during periods of economic downturn. Are there any infallible approaches for investing successfully in the stock market and acquiring undervalued shares? Only one. Will Rogers stated it when he said, "Buy some good stock and hold it. When it goes up, sell it. If it don't go up, don't buy it."

Costs of Investing in the Stock Market

All stocks and bonds are traded through brokers, whether the sale or purchase is done by an individual, a bank, a mutual fund, or an investment advisor. And whenever stocks and bonds are sold, a commission is paid to the broker. On

May 1, 1974, the New York Stock Exchange abolished its 183-year-old system of fixed brokerage commissions. Since that date, brokers' fees have been subject to negotiation.

An institutional investor, someone who manages a mutual fund or acts as an independent investment advisor to a number of individuals, or a trust department can negotiate lower fees because they are in a position to provide a much greater volume of business for a broker. If you are an individual investor who buys and sells on your own behalf, you have the choice of buying and selling stocks and bonds through either a so-called *full-service* brokerage firm or a *discount* brokerage firm. Full-service brokerage firms provide their customers with investment recommendations and other services. They must include the costs of these services in the commissions they charge. In contrast, discount brokerage firms generally provide no services other than the bare selling and buying of stocks and bonds as directed by you. Because they incur fewer costs, they are in a position to charge lower commissions.

When you purchase shares of stock through a full-service brokerage firm, you will pay a standard commission that ranges from 1.5 to 2.5 percent of the fair market value of the stock being bought or sold. Although the standard fee is determined in a more complicated fashion that relates to both the price of the shares and the number of shares being bought or sold, this is an accurate range for the commissions that you will pay, with 2 percent of the share price being about the average.

The broker's commission for bonds is generally a dollar amount per thousand. This too fluctuates, depending on a number of factors, but generally a fee of $15 to $20 per thousand is the average. Thus on a purchase of a $10,000 bond, the commission would be $150 to $200.

A discount brokerage firm charges approximately 50 percent less than would be charged on the same sale or purchase through a full-service brokerage firm.

Brokers' commissions are the only absolute cost that you must pay when you buy and sell stocks and bonds. However, in addition to the brokerage expenses, investors often incur additional costs. If you hire an independent investment advisor or an independent trust department, you pay, in addition to brokerage commissions, a fee for the advisor's services in making investment recommendations or investment decisions. However, because of the volume of their business, advisors may pay (and charge to you) lower commissions than you would otherwise be charged were you buying and selling on your own.

Professional Investment Advisors

Many professional investment advisors—both individuals and investment firms—provide their clients with quality stock and bond investment advice and recommendations. The problem here lies in identifying the "professional investment advisor." Only those individuals and institutions that charge for their services on a fee basis for investing and managing your money should be called professional investment advisors. These advisors are most likely to understand your philosophy and attitude about investing, know your goals and objectives, and make investments consistent with them. They are realistic. They do not make promises in an attempt to promote and sell a particular investment.

Fee-basis financial advisors charge an annual fee based on a percentage of the fair market value of the assets they have managed. This fee, which is negotiated between you and the investment advisor, generally ranges from 1 to 1.5 percent per annum. For example, an investment advisor who manages a $1 million portfolio that consists of stocks, bonds, and money market funds will charge an annual fee of from $10,000 to $15,000.

Numerous studies and attempts to evaluate the quality of investment advice have determined that the best investment advice comes from independent professional advisory individuals and firms. Unfortunately, many of them are unwilling to manage a portfolio unless its value is at least $250,000.

Bank trust departments are included within the definition of professional investment advisors. Trust departments charge on a fee basis for investing and reinvesting the assets subject to their control. Those who rate independent professional advisors generally rate the performance of bank trust departments below that of the independent advisors. You generally pay independent investment advisors more for their services than trust departments. This does not mean that there are not some very able and capable people in various trust departments. But it may be one reason why the overall result of independent investment advisors is better than most trust departments.

Banks are often charged with being too conservative in their investment approaches, but this is not an entirely fair charge. Independent investment advisors can be more aggressive in their investment decisions if that is a client's objective. Trust departments have a greater obligation to balance the assets in a portfolio for both income beneficiaries and for those who will receive the trust when it terminates. Thus, their emphasis is often to invest both for those who are to receive income from the trust and for those who are to receive the principal upon the termination of the trust. Therefore, bank investment managers often select investments that provide for both income and the preservation of an estate rather than for growth only.

A number of individuals and institutions that provide investment advice and recommendations often create the impression that they are investment advisors. They are not. Brokerage firms, financial planners, insurance companies, and a host of other so-called financial or money-management institutions do not qualify as investment advisors, and you should never rely on them as such. These companies are not paid on a fee basis, but rather receive a commission based on the amount of "investment product" (stocks, bonds, limited partnerships, and mutual funds) that they sell to you, their client.

This does not mean that they do not provide helpful information or that the investment product they are promoting is bad. It does mean that the investor must remember that all the individuals in each of these professions are under tremendous pressure to perform and are therefore very oriented to short-term goals. This pressure, combined with the substantial commissions promoters receive on the sale of investment products, absolutely disqualifies such individuals and entities from claiming to be investment advisors.

Financial planners, including those who represent brokerage firms and insurance companies, commonly argue that they are capable of wearing both hats—that of an investment advisor and that of a promoter of investment products. This is unrealistic. There is a direct conflict between the best interest of the client and the economic interest of the promoter. Furthermore, many of these individuals who are holding themselves out as investment advisors have neither the knowledge nor the experience to be classified as such, even if they were charging on a fee basis.

An article discussing the role of financial planners in the October 8, 1984, issue of *Forbes* magazine states:

Everyone is in the financial planning business these days. Yet no industry is so unregulated, so dimly perceived, promises so much, but can often do so little—or so much harm. Not since the Middle Ages when monks peddled indulgences to the guilt ridden at Eastertide has there been such a demand for a product of such questionable value. . . . Why do investors get sucked into wild investment schemes promoted by financial planners? Because they fail to understand the basically conservative nature of real financial planning and the planners they go to are greedy. The planners' fat commissions on such investments as diamonds, shelters, and limited partnerships drive them to sell rather than advise.

However, an investment advisor charging on a fee basis and being independent does not guarantee that you are going to receive quality investment advice. You must make sure that the advisor understands and follows your investment objectives. In this way you assume the principal responsibility for the investment of your money.

The fact that stockbrokers and financial planners receive commissions on what they are attempting to promote does not mean that the investments they recommend are necessarily bad. But often promoters do not know much about the investment product they are promoting. Therefore taking control of your investments means that you never put your hard-earned money into any investment product sold solely on the advice or recommendation of a stockbroker or financial planner who will derive a direct economic benefit from its sale.

Mutual Funds

A mutual fund is an investment company that owns and manages a portfolio of stocks, bonds, and money market accounts and whose own shares are sold and traded on the stock exchange. These funds are often described as growth funds, growth and income funds, or only income funds. There are tax-free bond funds, penny stock funds, foreign stock funds, and funds that only hold stocks of specific industries, such as high-technology stock funds.

Mutual funds first gained popularity in the 1950s and 1960s when the stock market was making solid gains. During the 1970s, many investors in the stock market became disenchanted, and many of the mutual funds had more withdrawals and redemptions than they had investors buying into the fund.

Since the sudden upsurge in the stock and bond markets beginning in August of 1982 combined with the tremendous amounts of money set aside in IRAs and other retirement plans, there has been a strong resurgence of investors putting their money into mutual funds. There are now several thousand mutual funds of all kinds, with more being formed each day.

Those who invest in mutual funds do so because they believe their fund provides (1) professional management, (2) diversification among a variety of security holdings, and (3) the opportunity to invest a relatively small sum and acquire an interest in all the assets controlled by the fund.

Costs of Investing in Mutual Funds

What are the costs of investing in mutual funds? When you purchase an interest in a mutual fund, you are buying professional management of that fund. The costs of this management include fees paid to the fund manager, analysts, attorneys, and accountants; costs incurred for advertising; custodial costs; and brokerage commissions charged to the fund for buying and selling stocks and bonds. These expenses are paid out of the fund's assets, and because you own an interest in the fund, they are, in effect, paid by you.

Fees, Commissions, Loads, and No-Loads

When you buy shares in a mutual fund from a stockbroker or a financial planner, you pay commissions and fees when you acquire your interest in the fund, and you may also pay fees when you withdraw or sell your interest in that fund. The normal commission is as high as 8.5 percent, but for some funds it may be as low as 3 to 4 percent.

A *no-load* fund is an investment fund in which you deal directly with the fund. If there is no broker involved, you will pay no commission, although there will probably be a redemption fee when you sell your interest. But if you acquire an interest in a no-load fund through a stockbroker or financial planner, you should assume he or she will still receive a fee for the sale. Many investors are not aware of this and believe that because the mutual fund is a no-load, a fee or commission is not being paid. They are wrong.

The broker may get a fee or commission for a no-load sale by a payment directly from the fund. For a fund describing itself as no-load, this could be described as a "kickback" rather than a commission or fee. Because your broker's fee and the fees of all other brokers promoting the fund are paid out of the assets of the fund, they are really being paid by you.

Rating Mutual Funds

Mutual funds are evaluated and studied by many individuals and institutions. They report on those funds that are doing well and those that are doing poorly. Some contend that you should only invest in funds that have a long history of superior performance. Others feel that the most meaningful evaluation of a fund is its performance for only the past year or two.

In the early 1960s, Fred Carr established Enterprise Fund, which specialized in acquiring growth companies. During the mid-1960s, it was the only mutual fund to rank among the nation's top twenty-five mutual funds for six straight years. But when the economy slowed down in 1969, the growth companies led the slide. Enterprise Fund, which had increased in value 116 percent in 1967 and 44 percent in 1968, had a dismal performance in 1969 and did even worse in 1970.

The simple truth is that it is extremely difficult to evaluate the performance of mutual funds on either a short- or long-term basis. In an article in *Forbes* magazine, William Baldwin wrote that the Investment Company Institute, a company that represents the mutual fund industry, published favorable but misleading statistics about the performance of mutual funds. These statistics stated that in the ten-year period ending June 30, 1984, the Standard & Poor's Index of Stocks was up by 189 percent, but that common stock funds, on the average, rose 345 percent, almost twice as much, in the same period. Baldwin points out that the Investment Company Institute selected some funds and ignored others in preparing this report. He says that if a fund was in existence ten years ago but didn't make it, merged, or liquidated because of a poor record, it is not reflected in these figures. Baldwin cites an article written by University of Rochester Professor Michael Jensen in which Jensen rated mutual fund managers as doing no better than wild guessers over the 1945–1964 period.

In addition to the difficulty of evaluating the performance of mutual funds over time, numerous studies question whether mutual funds provide the average investor with either diversification or the best obtainable professional investment management. Many of these reports conclude that the results achieved by the majority of mutual funds do not differ appreciably from what would have been achieved by an unmanaged portfolio consisting of the same proportion of common stocks and bonds.

Former United States Senator Thomas McIntyre, appearing before the Senate Banking Committee, demonstrated that, by randomly throwing darts at a newspaper listing of securities on the New York Stock Exchange, he could choose stocks that would have outperformed almost all the mutual funds.

After exhaustive research on mutual fund performance in 1970, Professors Friend, Blum, and Crockett concluded, "Random portfolios of New York Stock Exchange stocks with equal investment in each stock performed on the average over the period (January 1960 through June 1968) better than mutual funds in the same class."

Another issue you will want to think about when you consider mutual funds is diversification. When you acquire an interest in a mutual fund, are you getting diversification, as assumed, or are you really investing in the abilities of an individual—the fund manager? Are you really putting your investment eggs in one basket?

Virtually every article addressing the issue of mutual funds and their advantages will talk of both diversification and the idea of letting a pro pick your investments. Your investment dollars are allotted among a number of investments chosen by the fund's manager. But these articles will also caution that there is a catch: you must pick the fund manager.

The December 1984 issue of *Money* magazine included a series of articles on professional money managers. One article, titled "Keeping It Simple With Mutual Funds," stated, "You must choose a mutual fund with care and then check up on the manager periodically to make sure he is doing a good job." Statements like this are, of course, pure nonsense. The truth is that neither you nor your broker or financial planner is going to check on the performance of the mutual fund until it is far too late. And isn't that the reason you invested in the fund in the first place? In addition to the commissions and costs, getting out of mutual funds that you are told are not performing has to be one of the quickest ways of diminishing your estate. It is short-term investing at its worst.

In *Fact,* a magazine on managing money, the author of one article stated, "Mutual funds have now come full circle from their original concept as all-purpose, balanced investments where professional portfolio managers took a generally conservative approach to managing money. Now it's different. Mutual funds are more narrowly focused; many are riskier and more volatile."

Diversification means that the overall risk from owning many stocks is less than the risk of holding a few stocks. Obviously, the fewer stocks you hold, the greater the injury when one does poorly. Even the small investor should work toward diversification. Robert Hagin and Chris Mader, in a book titled *The New Science of Investing,* argue that it is a myth that small investors cannot adequately diversify their holdings. They contend,

> It can be shown mathematically in fact that when your investments are spread among several stocks which are not related to each other overall, the risk will be reduced. And that five or six stocks selected for their offsetting risk characteristics will give a stability comparable to most mutual funds which invest hundreds of millions of dollars.

The conclusion is simple: As an investor acquiring individual blue chip stocks to be held over a long period of time, you will have more control over your investments and a better chance that your investments will outperform the average mutual fund.

The Bottom Line

When you combine the investment of your money with the investment of your time and effort and you have the knowledge and control over the activities of that investment, you can choose to be aggressive in your approach. As an active investor, you can "go for it."

But passive investors cannot make investments based on promises and wishful thinking. They must resist the temptation of trying to beat the market or trying to make a big score. They should buy quality products, whether stocks or fixed-income investments, and keep their long-term goals in mind.

CHAPTER 5

The Ultimate Tax Shelter: Poverty

Dr. Lam's accountant has just informed him that his income for the year is much greater than they estimated, and unless he creates some substantial tax deductions and credits that will reduce his taxable income for the year, he faces a large and unanticipated increase in the amount of taxes he will be required to pay.

Dr. Lam is concerned. But his fears will soon be put to rest when he discovers that there are investments available that promise to resolve his tax dilemma. Dr. Lam is now prey for promoters and salespeople who will capitalize on his emotional, often fanatical, desire to avoid taxes. These individuals will propose a *tax shelter* as the answer to Dr. Lam's current financial crisis.

What is a tax shelter? A tax shelter is a product of the Internal Revenue Code, which is the law enacted by Congress that establishes the rules by which you determine the amount of taxes you are required to pay to the federal government. This code tells you what you must include in your gross income, what expenses and credits will be allowed in arriving at your taxable income, and the percentage or bracket that you are in to determine the amount of tax that you will pay on your taxable income.

During the past fifty years, our tax system has been used not only to raise revenue to support and maintain our government and its programs, but also as a vehicle for prodding the economy. Congress has done this by providing us, the tax-payers, with deductions and credits as an incentive for making certain kinds of investments.

When you receive a tax credit, you get a dollar-for-dollar reduction of your tax liability to the extent of the amount of that credit. For example, if you purchase an asset that costs $10,000 and you are entitled to a 10 percent credit, then you apply that credit amount ($1,000) to directly reduce your tax liability. If your tax liability before the credit was $5,000, your tax liability after the credit will be $4,000.

A deduction reduces your tax liability, but it is not as good as a credit. A deduction is an amount that will reduce the gross income amount you use to arrive at your taxable income. For example, if you pay $1,000 in interest during the year, you will deduct that amount from your gross income in arriving at your taxable income. And if you are in a 50 percent tax bracket, the effect of this deduction is that you will pay $500 less in taxes.

A tax shelter is frequently an interest in a limited partner-ship that has purchased assets that provide both deductions and credits to the investor and limited partner. When you make such an investment, you receive the immediate benefit of these deductions and credits on your tax return. Usually, the limited partnership itself produces little, if any, income; therefore these deductions and credits are applied against your other income. It is in this sense that you "shelter" income that would otherwise be subject to tax.

Tax shelters are investments that generate tax credits and deductions that the limited partners take against their incomes. In this way the government encourages investments. Oil and gas exploration, real estate, and a host of other investments from time to time hold this preferred status given by the government.

If the only reason you are investing your money in a tax shelter is to offset the income you earned during the year, then the tax shelter makes little sense. In Gus Arriola's comic strip, "Gordo," Gordo is told that Jones may not be able to play golf anymore. "What a shame," he says. "He would have made big money!" Gordo's friend responds, "And pay big taxes?" "Oh, there are tax shelters!" says Gordo. His friend responds, "Ha! Jones already have best loophole of everybody! No work!"

Jones is right. You would be better spending your time on more enjoyable pursuits rather than working to earn income that you later pay to someone else in the form of an investment, the sole purpose of which is to eliminate the income you always thought was so necessary to maintain your standard of living.

The creation, development, and promotion of tax shelters increased dramatically during the 1970s and into the 1980s. Shelters have become an extremely lucrative business for those who put them together and promote them. In fact, a large part of the initial write-off in virtually every tax shelter results from promoters' fees, interest expense, and other fees paid to developers and institutions that financed the shelter.

Tax shelters are formed by individuals or corporations called *syndicators*. The syndicators acquire the assets that are sold to the limited partnership. Many times these properties are sold at very inflated prices. When you acquire an interest in such a partnership, 8 to 10 percent of your investment goes to the firm that sold it to you. Management fees, some quoted to be as high as 32 percent, are paid by the investors. Furthermore, there are annual fees and operating expenses. If the properties are later sold, the promoters take an average of 18 percent of the purchase price.

In addition to the fees and costs that are paid out of your investment dollars, the potential gain from the investment is often based on economic projections that assume unrealistically high rates of inflation, which are relied upon to increase the value of the asset owned by the limited partnership. And although such inflation did occur during the late 1970s, there is every indication that it can no longer be relied upon to "bail out" what are basically poor investments.

Each day, newspapers throughout the country carry stories of individuals who lost substantial sums of money by investing in tax shelters that were simply fraudulent. Four promoters in New York were recently convicted of conspiring to supply investors with more than $130 million worth of phony tax shelters in 1979 and 1980. Their clients reportedly included many wealthy celebrities, most of whom were in the entertainment business and were certainly able to hire sophisticated and qualified investment and tax advisors.

Another article cited a tax attorney practicing in Beverly Hills, California, who promised his clients that the investments he was promoting were approved by the IRS and would accrue both tax benefits and profits. Shortly thereafter, the attorney's law firm dissolved; his former clients are now attempting to defend their deductions in court while gaining invaluable insights into the strategies and costs of tax litigation.

The classic case of the promoter gone awry is that of William Green, who offered a series of seminars on "How to Pay No More Taxes Legally." He was recently reported as an escapee from the U.S. Bureau of Prisons, having failed to return to a community release unit at the Chicago Federal Metropolitan Correction Center. It can be assumed that all future seminars will be canceled until further notice.

Many tax shelters, although not fraudulent, are simply lousy investments. In financial writer Jane Bryant Quinn's article "Honest Tax Shelters Seldom Are Worth the Money," she commented on the promises and guarantees given by the promoters of a tax-sheltered investment at a time when they knew that the promised deductions and credits were being challenged by the IRS.

Dan Dorfman, another financial commentator, wrote an article about the real estate shelters sold in 1983. He noted that taxpayers will invest up to $12 billion in these shelters (estimated to be $18 billion to $20 billion for 1984) and won't know for several years (because their income-tax returns are not audited until then) whether they will receive the promised tax benefits. Dorfman quoted Mark Steinberg, the head of tax-sheltered investments at Boetcher & Company, as saying, "We wouldn't touch most real estate deals offered by syndicators and a number of brokerage firms because they are mediocre; inflated prices are being paid because of bidding wars for property, and investors are in for big disappointments." Steinberg advised that, before you invest in a tax shelter, determine whether the property was bought at a realistic price and whether the project is economically feasible and determine the fees the syndicators are being paid.

This is excellent advice. Unfortunately, because of the size and complexity of most syndications and the limited expense you as an investor are willing to incur in checking out these investments, it is virtually impossible for you to follow his recommendation. And even if you made an effort to do so, this information is not easily available to you or is difficult to verify. Although those who promote these investments to their clients often talk as though they are knowledgeable about them, the truth is that they often know virtually nothing about the product.

If tax shelters are such poor investments, why do they have such appeal? There are several good reasons for this. First, a tax shelter is a form of instant gratification. Because most of us find it difficult to save, it is easy to accept the argument that we are doing so by investing our money in a way that is guaranteed to produce a tax loss. If you reduce your taxes, aren't you saving money? The answer, of course, is that you don't save anything when you withdraw your money from your savings account or borrow it so that you can give these dollars to the promoter of the tax shelter, rather than pay a part of it to the government in the form of taxes. The fact that the saving is illusory and defies logic and common sense is not important. It is easier to talk to a teenager in love than to someone who is about to embark on his first tax-sheltered investment, with its promise of immediate and substantial tax savings and the remote possibility that it will prove to be a worthwhile investment.

Tax shelter promoters also capitalize on the myths about the wealthy and how their estates were acquired. These myths are perpetuated by magazines and books that reveal "the easy way" to create an estate. Even responsible magazines do this with the hope of increasing their circulation. Just such an article was offered by *Newsweek* in April 1984: "How Americans Beat the Tax Man—Welcome to the Wild World of Tax Shelters Where Almost Everyone Can Profit—Except the Treasury." *Newsweek* said that tax shelters are a national shell game. "Where the shells are tax deductible, both the player and the sponsor can win—and only the government is left to figure out where the money went." It concluded that the rewards of playing this game will continue to outweigh the risks. What *Newsweek* failed to learn is that those who invest in these tax shelters are often more perplexed about where the money went than is the government.

Unfortunately, literature promoting tax shelters is often misleading and designed to give investors a false sense of security. The brochure that explains the benefits of an investment and its tax advantages often carries the opinions of prestigious law firms, established national accounting firms, banks, and other well-known financial institutions. Would such reputable firms and organizations be associated with or endorse an investment in a limited partnership if they were not entirely satisfied as to its worthiness? Unfortunately, the answer is clearly "yes."

Furthermore, the literature is often quite limited, and the articles do not address the economics of the investment. They only deal with the technical aspects of whether an investment appears to qualify for certain tax benefits or meets some other requirement of state or federal law. Judge Henry Friendly, of the United States Court of Appeals, summed up the problem for investors who rely on these opinions in a decision in which he stated, "In our complex society, the accountant's certificate and the lawyer's opinion can be instruments for inflicting a pecuniary loss far more important than the chisel and the crowbar." In other words, in determining whether a tax shelter is a good or bad investment, these opinions don't mean a thing.

So when does a tax sheltered investment make sense? It makes sense when it is first evaluated as a good investment— and one with tax advantages. The tax benefits from depreciation, depletion, capital gains, tax-free income, and tax credits and the deductibility of payments to IRAs and Keogh and corporate retirement plans are considerations that bear on every investment we make and are important building blocks in creating an estate. For example, the decision of whether to buy or rent a home will often be resolved in favor of buying because the property taxes and interest payments (which constitute the bulk of the early payments) are deductible against income, whereas rental payments are not. Thus, the costs of owning property are less than those of renting it.

Another excellent example is the establishment of an IRA account or a Keogh plan. Contributions to these plans are encouraged because they are deductions against income. They are excellent tax shelters, not only because they provide the tax incentive for making the contribution, but more important, because they also provide an opportunity to invest in and control assets in which the income will not be taxed but can be reinvested until such time as it is withdrawn. The accumulation and reinvestment of this income from such investments provides us the opportunity to accumulate an estate at a much faster rate than would otherwise be possible.

Minimizing taxes is important. Investing wisely is essential. However, when the only reason for making the investment is the immediate tax benefit accompanied by a vague hope that the capital may be returned at some date in the future, then the tax tail is wagging the investment dog. And for the passive investor, such investments jeopardize capital and reduce the resources that would otherwise be available to create an estate and provide security and a higher standard of living.

CHAPTER 6

Investment Strategies

It wasn't raining when Noah built the Ark.
Howard Ruff

The king gathered together his wise men and commanded them to give him a statement that would be true for all times and on all occasions. After much thought and debate, they returned to tell him they had succeeded. He asked them, "Tell me, what is it?" They said, "And this too shall pass." And so it is with investment strategies.

Investment strategies vary because of changes in the economy that bear favorably or unfavorably on any particular kind of investment. This has been demonstrated by the changes that have occurred in the economy during the past fifty years, if not the past ten. The period of 1975 to 1980 was one of high inflation and the belief that it would continue. However, five years later in 1985, the philosophy and outlook had changed to one of deflation. These changes directly affected the values of real property, common stocks, bonds, and all other investments.

Our personal investment objectives change as we grow older from that of accumulating an estate to that of preserving capital and providing a source of income for our retirement. As our objectives change, so must our strategies. Because we have limited resources to invest, we must avoid making bad investments—investments born out of greed and nurtured by false hopes. The illusion of a quick and easy profit is the principal enemy of a sound investment strategy. Recognizing our human vulnerability for these kinds of investments is a first step toward developing a sensible investment strategy.

CREATING AN ESTATE

An estate is created by investing the income from your earnings and by reinvesting the income received from your investments. Adam Smith, the famous Scottish economist, said, "Parsimony and not industry is the immediate cause of the increase of capital. But whatever industry might acquire, if parsimony did not save and store up, the capital would never be the greater." In other words, it's not how much you make that will determine the size of your estate, but rather how much you save, how early you begin, and how wisely you invest.

That this is difficult is evidenced by the sad fact that 95 percent of all Americans who reach sixty-five years of age cannot provide for their own support. They must rely on public and private assistance, or they must continue to work. Many are required to rely solely on Social Security. This is certainly a revealing statistic about the people who reside in the land of opportunity.

The only other way an estate is created is from the appreciation in the value of your investments—your assets. You buy real estate, common stocks, gold, and silver for their anticipated appreciation. A recent newspaper article titled "Pasting Up a Pint-Size Fortune" provides one example of accumulating an estate in this manner. An investor who had purchased a one-of-a-kind British Guiana stamp for $280,000 in 1970 sold the stamp in 1980 for $935,000. If you had purchased a home in the San Francisco Bay Area in the mid-1960s for

$25,000, it probably had a value of at least $200,000 by 1985. This is an eightfold increase in your original investment over a twenty-year period.

However, there is no guarantee that assets will appreciate in value, so the only sure method of creating an estate is to consume less of your income in an attempt to save more. In fact, this is a necessary first step. Unfortunately, many investors do not realize the potential of creating an estate in this manner. They prefer to believe that they will someday hit it big. But whatever your approach, understanding the concept of compound interest will make you far more aware of the inherent potential in your choice of investments.

UNDERSTANDING COMPOUND INTEREST

The Baron de Rothschild, one of the wealthiest men in the world, was once asked to name the seven wonders of the world. He is reported to have answered, "I cannot, but I know that the eighth is compound interest."

In its simplest form, compound interest means that the interest you receive from the loan of your money is itself reinvested so that it becomes capital and as such produces additional interest, which is also reinvested, and so on. This consistent increase in your capital as you continue to reinvest the interest income results from the buildup—the compounding—of your interest.

The Rule of 72

The rule of 72 can be used to anticipate the future size of your estate based on the reinvestment of income. It will also help you compare the potential appreciation in various investment choices. If you divide the rate of interest you are receiving on your investment into 72, and if you assume that you will be able to reinvest the income at that rate of interest, you can easily determine the number of years that it will take for your investment to double in value.

For example, assume you purchased a $10,000 bond that pays 10 percent interest and is due and payable in ten years. You know that you will receive $1,000 interest each year during the ten-year period until the bond is paid and you receive your $10,000 principal. If you divide the rate of interest (10 percent) into 72, and if you assume that the $1,000 of interest you receive each year will also be reinvested at 10 percent interest, then you know that your principal will double approximately every 7.2 years (72/10 = 7.2). If you assume that you continue to reinvest each year's interest at 10 percent per annum, you know that in 21.6 years your original investment of $10,000 will increase to $80,000. You know this because you know that your $10,000 investment will double every 7.2 years. Thus, your $10,000 doubles to $20,000 in the first 7.2 years; your $20,000 doubles to $40,000 in the next 7.2 years; and your $40,000 doubles to $80,000 in the next 7.2 years.

The "miracle" of compound interest is further illustrated by extending this example for an additional 21.6 years. Your $80,000 will double to $160,000 in the next 7.2 years; your $160,000 will double to $320,000 in the following 7.2 years; and your $320,000 would then double to $640,000 in the next 7.2 years. Thus, in 21.6 years, your investment increased eight times, and in 43.2 years, your investment increased sixty-four times—all this from a single investment of $10,000.

Compound interest is a method of comparing the growth of all investments. For example, is the Guiana stamp that increased its value more than three times in ten years a better investment than the house that increased eightfold from $25,000 to $200,000 in twenty years? The stamp increased at an annual compound interest rate of 12.8 percent, while the home only increased at an annual compound interest rate of 11.0 percent.

The Problem in Creating an Estate from the Reinvestment of Income

Compound interest provides for the reliable increase of wealth, and interest rates on high-quality fixed-term investments have ranged from 10 to 17 percent between 1975 and 1985, with particularly high interest rates from 1980 to 1985. So why haven't more people invested the bulk of their assets in interest-bearing instruments that guarantee this constant and substantial buildup of their capital? There are two principal reasons:

1. Tax laws. Interest on bonds, money market funds, and bank accounts and notes is taxed as ordinary income. Thus the numbers do not work when the federal and state governments grab a substantial portion of that income before it can be reinvested. But when an asset appreciates in value, the appreciation is not taxed until the asset is later sold.

2. Inflation. A fixed-income investment may provide a substantial amount of interest, but the principal amount does not change. If you pay $10,000 and purchase a ten-year bond, you will receive your interest; but at the end of the period, your bond is worth just $10,000. However, if inflation continues as it has in the past, that $10,000 received ten years later will have perhaps one-half or one-third of the purchasing power of the original $10,000 used to acquire the bond. But assets with appreciation potential can increase in value to keep pace with inflation.

Most people don't really understand the concept of compound interest and give tax laws and inflation as reasons for not applying it to the creation of an estate. As a result, if they have an opportunity to make an equity investment that may increase in value threefold in ten years, they may not be aware that this increase represents a compound rate of interest that may be less than they could achieve by fixed-income investments.

That many investors don't fully understand the miracle of compound interest is best demonstrated by the often unfortunate choice of investments in qualified retirement plans.

Applying the Compound Interest Concept to Investments in a Qualified Retirement Plan

Qualified retirement plans, whether corporate pension and profit sharing plans, partnership and individual Keogh plans, or IRAs, play an increasingly important role in your efforts to accumulate an estate. You can contribute various amounts to these plans, depending on the type you establish.

The major incentive for establishing these plans is that amounts you pay into the plan are tax deductible. And the income generated from the investment in a qualified plan is reinvested and not taxed until a future date, when you begin making withdrawals from the plan. At that time, you will be taxed on the income. And when you receive payments from the plan, the income tax consequences of these payments will be the same whether the assets accumulated in the plan resulted from the reinvestment of income or from the appreciation in the value of the assets.

Thus, all investments in a qualified retirement plan, whether they produce income only (bonds), a combination of income and growth (common stocks), or growth only (gold), are treated as *growth investments*. In other words, whichever investment choice has the greatest potential for increase in value over the period of time that it is held in the plan, considering the full reinvestment of the income, is the best investment.

This concept is best illustrated by the investment choices available to every person who establishes an IRA. The government, in an effort to promote economic independence among the American people, created this type of retirement plan to provide every working American with the opportunity to make his or her retirement years far more comfortable than they might otherwise be. Keep in mind that much greater amounts are allowable for contribution to Keogh and corporate plans. The maximum contribution an individual can make from his or her earnings to an IRA is $2,000 per year. A married couple with only one spouse working can contribute an additional $250, for a total of $2,250 per year. A married couple with both spouses working can contribute up to $4,000 per year. These provisions are subject to legislative changes in existing regulations.

To illustrate the effect of compound interest on an IRA (or in any other kind of qualified retirement plan), Table 1 shows the amount you would accumulate if you invested $2,500 each year in an interest-bearing investment and continually reinvested the interest from that investment at a constant rate of 8 percent, 10 percent, or 12 percent. Table 1 shows that if you save consistently over a period of time and reinvest your income, even at 8 percent interest, you will greatly add to your security and standard of living during your retirement years.

The two most important factors in achieving the maximum benefits of compound interest are (1) the period of time during which the interest is reinvested and (2) the rate at which the interest is reinvested. The importance of time and the rate of interest is illustrated in Tables 2, 3, and 4. In these

TABLE 1

Compounding Interest

Number of Years	Total Amount Contributed at $2,500 per Year	Value of IRA at End of Given Number of Years Assuming Interest Reinvested		
		8%	10%	12%
10	$ 25,000	$ 39,114	$ 43,828	$ 49,136
15	37,500	73,311	87,374	104,383
20	50,000	123,557	157,506	201,747
25	62,500	197,386	270,454	373,335
30	75,000	305,865	452,359	675,732
35	87,500	465,255	745,317	1,208,658
40	100,000	699,453	1,217,130	2,147,856

tables, it is assumed that Pat Early contributed $2,000 a year to an IRA between the ages of twenty-two and thirty. Chris Slow began making contributions at age thirty-one and made a contribution each year until age sixty-five. Table 2 compares the results when interest is reinvested at 8 percent, Table 3 compares the results when interest is reinvested at 10 percent, and Table 4 compares the results when interest is reinvested at 12 percent.

But the advantages of an IRA, a Keogh, or a corporate retirement plan do not end with the amounts you acquire at the time you retire. Although you have various options as to how you wish to draw the amounts from these accounts, if you withdraw only a portion of the account, the balance continues to generate income that is not taxed but reinvested and added to capital.

Under the existing tax laws, you can begin withdrawing from your IRA at age fifty-nine and a half without any tax penalty, and you can draw out as much as you choose. But you are not required to begin withdrawing from your IRA until age seventy and a half. If you wait until age seventy and a half, the Internal Revenue Service has some rather complicated rules to determine how quickly you must deplete your IRA. Essentially, the purpose of these rules is to require that the full amount of your IRA be withdrawn over the period

TABLE 2

Contribution at Beginning of Year—Interest at 8% per Annum

	Pat Early		Chris Slow	
Age	Contribution	Balance at End of Year	Contribution	Balance at End of Year
22	$2,000	$ 2,160	0	0
23	2,000	4,493	0	0
24	2,000	7,012	0	0
25	2,000	9,733	0	0
26	2,000	12,672	0	0
27	2,000	15,846	0	0
28	2,000	19,273	0	0
29	2,000	22,975	0	0
30	2,000	26,973	0	0
31	0	29,131	$2,000	$ 2,160
32	0	31,461	2,000	4,493
33	0	33,978	2,000	7,012
34	0	36,697	2,000	9,733
35	0	39,632	2,000	12,672
36	0	42,803	2,000	15,846
37	0	46,227	2,000	19,273
38	0	49.925	2,000	22,975
39	0	53,919	2,000	26,973
40	0	58,233	2,000	31,291
41	0	62,892	2,000	35,954
42	0	67,923	2,000	40,991
43	0	73,357	2,000	46,430
44	0	79,225	2,000	52,304
45	0	85,563	2,000	58,649
46	0	92,408	2,000	65,500
47	0	99,801	2,000	72,900
48	0	107,785	2,000	80,893
49	0	116,408	2,000	89,524
50	0	125,721	2,000	98,846
51	0	135,778	2,000	108,914
52	0	146,640	2,000	119,787
53	0	158,372	2,000	131,530
54	0	171,041	2,000	144,212
55	0	184,725	2,000	157,909
56	0	199,503	2,000	172,702
57	0	215,463	2,000	188,678
58	0	232,700	2,000	205,932
59	0	251,316	2,000	224,566
60	0	271,421	2,000	244,692
61	0	293,135	2,000	266,427
62	0	316,586	2,000	289,901
63	0	341,913	2,000	315,253
64	0	369,266	2,000	342,634
65	0	398,807	2,000	372,204

TABLE 3

Contribution at Beginning of Year—Interest at 10% per Annum

	Pat Early		Chris Slow	
Age	Contribution	Balance at End of Year	Contribution	Balance at End of Year
22	$2,000	$ 2,200	0	0
23	2,000	4,620	0	0
24	2,000	7,282	0	0
25	2,000	10,210	0	0
26	2,000	13,431	0	0
27	2,000	16,974	0	0
28	2,000	20,872	0	0
29	2,000	25,159	0	0
30	2,000	29,875	0	0
31	0	32,862	$2,000	$ 2,200
32	0	36,149	2,000	4,620
33	0	39,763	2,000	7,282
34	0	43,740	2,000	10,210
35	0	48,114	2,000	13,431
36	0	52,925	2,000	16,974
37	0	58,218	2,000	20,872
38	0	64,039	2,000	25,159
39	0	70,443	2,000	29,875
40	0	77,488	2,000	35,062
41	0	85,236	2,000	40,769
42	0	93,760	2,000	47,045
43	0	103,136	2,000	53,950
44	0	113,450	2,000	61,545
45	0	124,795	2,000	69,899
46	0	137,274	2,000	79,089
47	0	151,002	2,000	89,198
48	0	166,102	2,000	100,318
49	0	182,712	2,000	112,550
50	0	200,983	2,000	126,005
51	0	221,081	2,000	140,805
52	0	243,189	2,000	157,086
53	0	267,508	2,000	174,995
54	0	294,259	2,000	194,694
55	0	323,685	2,000	216,364
56	0	356,054	2,000	240,200
57	0	391,659	2,000	266,420
58	0	430,825	2,000	295,262
59	0	473,908	2,000	326,988
60	0	521,298	2,000	361,887
61	0	573,428	2,000	400,276
62	0	630,771	2,000	442,503
63	0	693,848	2,000	488,953
04	0	763,233	2,000	540,049
65	0	839,556	2,000	506,251

TABLE 4

Contribution at Beginning of Year—Interest at 12% per Annum

	Pat Early		Chris Slow	
Age	Contribution	Balance at End of Year	Contribution	Balance at End of Year
22	$2,000	$ 2,240	0	0
23	2,000	4,749	0	0
24	2,000	7,559	0	0
25	2,000	10,706	0	0
26	2,000	14,230	0	0
27	2,000	18,178	0	0
28	2,000	22,599	0	0
29	2,000	27,551	0	0
30	2,000	33,097	0	0
31	0	37,069	$2,000	$ 2,240
32	0	41,517	2,000	4,749
33	0	46,500	2,000	7,559
34	0	52,080	2,000	10,706
35	0	58,329	2,000	14,230
36	0	65,329	2,000	18,178
37	0	73,168	2,000	22,599
38	0	81,948	2,000	27,551
39	0	91,782	2,000	33,097
40	0	102,796	2,000	39,309
41	0	115,131	2,000	46,266
42	0	128,947	2,000	54,058
43	0	144,421	2,000	62,785
44	0	161,751	2,000	72,559
45	0	181,161	2,000	00,507
46	0	202,901	2,000	95,767
47	0	227,249	2,000	109,499
48	0	254,518	2,000	124,879
49	0	285,061	2,000	142,105
50	0	319,268	2,000	161,397
51	0	357,580	2,000	183,005
52	0	400,490	2,000	207,206
53	0	448,548	2,000	234,310
54	0	502,374	2,000	264,668
55	0	562,659	2,000	298,668
56	0	630,178	2,000	336,748
57	0	705,800	2,000	379,398
58	0	790,496	2,000	427,166
59	0	885,355	2,000	480,665
60	0	991,598	2,000	540,585
61	0	1,110,589	2,000	607,695
62	0	1,243,860	2,000	682,859
63	0	1,393,123	2,000	767,042
64	0	1,560,298	2,000	861,327
65	0	1,747,534	2,000	966,926

of your life expectancy. If you are married, it must be with-drawn over the joint life expectancy of you and your spouse. For example, a female aged sixty-five has a life expectancy of approximately eighteen years. A married couple with the male spouse seventy years of age and the female spouse sixty-six years has a joint life expectancy of approximately twenty years.

Table 5 assumes that a sixty-five-year-old female has accumulated approximately $300,000 in her IRA and that her remaining investments in the IRA continue to produce income at the rate of 8 percent per annum. This table illustrates the amount she will withdraw if at age sixty-five she begins withdrawing from her IRA the minimum amounts required to be withdrawn under the Internal Revenue Code (you can always

TABLE 5

$306,000 at Age 65

Year	Age	Fraction Withdrawn	Withdrawal at End of Year	8% Earnings on Balance in IRA	Value of Principal Remaining in IRA
1	65	1/18	$ 17,000.00	$24,480.00	$313,480.00
2	66	1/17	18,440.00	25,078.40	320,118.40
3	67	1/16	20,007.40	25,609.47	325,720.47
4	68	1/15	21,714.70	26,057.64	330,063.41
5	69	1/14	23,575.96	26,405.07	332,892.52
6	70	1/13	25,607.12	26,631.40	333,916.80
7	71	1/12	27,826.40	26,713.34	332,803.74
8	72	1/11	30,254.89	26,624.30	329,173.15
9	73	1/10	32,917.32	26,333.85	322,589.68
10	74	1/9	35,843.30	25,807.17	312,553.55
11	75	1/8	39,069.19	25,004.28	298,488.64
12	76	1/7	42,641.23	23,879.09	279,726.50
13	77	1/6	46,621.08	22,378.12	255,483.54
14	78	1/5	51,096.71	20,438.68	224,825.51
15	79	1/4	56,206.38	17,986.04	186,605.17
16	80	1/3	62,201.72	14,928.41	139,331.86
17	81	1/2	69,665.93	11,146.55	80,812.48
18	82	Balance	80,812.48		
			$701,501.81		

draw more). Thus, on a total investment of $75,000 made at the rate of $2,500 a year for thirty years, you would draw out a total of $701,500 from your IRA.

Table 6 assumes that you have accumulated $675,000 in your IRA (thirty years of annual contributions of $2,500 reinvested at 12 percent per annum) and that your investments remaining in the IRA continue to produce income at the rate of 12 percent per annum. This table illustrates the amount you will withdraw if at age seventy you begin drawing from your IRA the minimum amounts required by the Internal Revenue Code under the joint life expectancy rules.

TABLE 6

$675,000 at Age 70

Year	Age	Fraction Withdrawn	Withdrawal at End of Year	12% Earnings on Balance in IRA	Value of Principal Remaining in IRA
1	70	1/20	$ 33,750.00	$ 81,000.00	$ 722,250.00
2	71	1/19	38,013.16	86,670.00	770,900.84
3	72	1/18	42,828.16	92,508.82	820,587.50
4	73	1/17	48,269.85	98,470.50	870,788.15
5	74	1/16	54,424.26	104,494.58	920,858.47
6	75	1/15	61,390.56	110,503.02	969,970.93
7	76	1/14	69,283.64	116,396.51	1,017,083.80
8	77	1/13	78,237.22	122,050.06	1,060,896.64
9	78	1/12	88,408.05	127,307.60	1,099,796.19
10	79	1/11	99,981.47	131,975.54	1,131,790.26
11	80	1/10	113,179.03	135,814.83	1,154,426.06
12	81	1/9	128,269.56	138,531.13	1,164,687.63
13	82	1/8	145,585.95	139,762.52	1,158,864.20
14	83	1/7	165,552.03	139,063.70	1,132,375.87
15	84	1/6	188,729.31	135,885.10	1,079,531.66
16	85	1/5	215,906.33	129,543.80	993,169.13
17	86	1/4	248,292.28	119,180.30	864,057.15
18	87	1/3	288,019.05	103,686.86	679,724.96
19	88	1/2	339,862.48	81,567.00	421,429.48
20	89	Balance	421,429.48		421,429.48
			$2,869,411.87		

An additional advantage you gain by withdrawing money from a retirement plan over the period of your life expectancy is that the amounts you withdraw increase each year. This method protects you against inflation in the event that the cost of living continues to rise during your retirement years. This can be extremely important in maintaining your standard of living.

Locking In Compound Interest—A Zero-Interest Bond

When you buy a high-quality interest-bearing bond for a twenty-year period, you know the rate of interest you will receive on that investment each year during that twenty-year period. However, if you apply the concept of compound interest and want to determine how large your capital will be in twenty years, you must assume that you can reinvest that income at a specific rate of interest. Because interest rates increase and decrease, it is impossible to accurately predict the amount of interest buildup over a given period of time. This is not true when you purchase a *zero-interest bond*.

As discussed in Chapter 3, a bond is a loan of your money at a given rate of interest for a given period of time. A zero-interest bond is still a loan of your money for a given period of time, but you do not receive any interest during that period of time. Instead, the interest is calculated each year and added to the principal of your bond, thus giving you the benefit of compound interest until the due date of the bond. On the due date of the bond, you receive the principal amount of your bond and all the interest that accumulated over the period of time you held the bond.

Obviously, if you can buy a $10,000 bond that pays 15 percent interest per annum, and you can buy a $10,000 bond in which all interest is accumulated and paid to you upon the maturity of the bond, you would expect to receive a much greater amount on this latter type of bond. And you will. You know that, based on the rule of 72, if you are receiving 14.5 percent interest per annum on an investment and you reinvested that interest at that same constant rate, your investment would double approximately every five years. Thus, your $10,000 zero-interest bond would double to $20,000 in five years; your $20,000 would double to $40,000 in the next five years; your $40,000 would double to $80,000 in the next five years; and your $80,000 would double to $160,000 in the next five years. Your investment would increase sixteen times over the twenty-year period that you held the bond.

This is exactly the investment that Merrill Lynch Pierce Fenner & Smith offered to the investing public in August of 1982. Investors were told that $100,000 in their zero-interest bond fund would pay $1,600,000 in twenty years. Furthermore (because they were acquiring U.S. Treasury obligations for the fund), Merrill Lynch offered the public an investment that was backed by the full faith and credit of the United States government.

There are, however, both advantages and risks to acquiring a zero-interest bond instead of an interest-paying bond. The zero-interest bond is far more volatile. The market value of a zero-interest bond is more affected (either up or down) by changes in the interest rates than a bond that pays interest each year. This is significant if you want to sell a zero-interest bond before its maturity.

Assume you purchase a $10,000 bond that pays interest at the rate of 10 percent per annum with a twenty-year maturity. This means that each year during the twenty-year period, you would receive $1,000 of interest income. If, during that period, the interest rates increase to 13 percent, you would be able to reinvest your $1,000-a-year interest income at the higher rate. If, however, the interest rates dropped to 7 percent per annum, you could only reinvest that interest at the lower rate.

Because a zero-interest bond does not pay out regular interest but rather, in effect, compounds at the constant rate current at the time you acquired the bond, you are locked in for the twenty-year period of time—for better or worse. If interest rates increase during that period of time, you cannot take advantage of reinvesting at the higher rates because you do not receive interest payments. If interest rates drop (as they have dramatically since August of 1982, when Merrill Lynch first offered the zero-interest bond), you would be locked in a higher and more favorable rate of interest.

ACQUIRING STOCKS IN YOUR RETIREMENT PLAN

The growth potential of bonds in a retirement plan is based on the reinvestment of income. The growth potential of common stocks is based on the reinvestment of the dividends and the appreciation in the value of the stock. It is this appreciation and the increased amount of dividends that make common stocks an attractive long-range investment.

When common stocks increase in value, it is generally because of higher corporate earnings, or at least the anticipation that this will occur. And when it does, the corporation will then declare larger dividends. Thus, the return on your original investment continues to increase as a corporation increases its dividend payout.

In his book *Super Stocks,* Ken Fisher says that if you had purchased IBM stock at its low in 1932 and sold it at the very top of the market in 1956, you would have made a small fortune. If you had bought the stock at $52.50 per share and held it for approximately twenty-five years, you would have sold it for $550 per share. This is approximately ten times your original investment over a twenty-five-year period.

The reinvestment of stock dividends, like the reinvestment of interest income, adds dramatically to the long-term value of common-stock investments. If in 1926 you had purchased an equal amount of all the stocks on the New York Stock Exchange and had reinvested all subsequent dividends, by 1966 your original investment would have multiplied thirty-five times. However, had you not reinvested the dividends, the value of your portfolio would have increased six times.

The 1984 annual report of the Washington Mutual Investors Fund, a fund invested primarily in blue chip American stocks, showed the results of investing $10,000 in the fund on May 1, 1954, by computing its value on April 30, 1984. If all dividends had been taken in cash, your stocks would have increased to $86,011 over the thirty-year period. However, if the dividends had been reinvested in the fund rather than paid out, your $10,000 investment would have increased to $297,385. Thus, approximately two-thirds of this value is due to the reinvestment of the dividends. Ten thousand dollars invested in the fund during that thirty-year period, with all dividends reinvested, increased at an annual compound interest rate of 11.97 percent.

SOME CONSIDERATIONS REGARDING FIXED-TERM INVESTMENTS IN A QUALIFIED RETIREMENT PLAN

From Table 1, we know that if you could be given a guarantee that all your money invested in a retirement plan compounded at an annual rate of between 8 and 12 percent over an extended period of time, you would be assured of having a substantial sum in that account at your retirement date.

When long-term interest rates on treasury bonds are 9 percent or more per annum, these bonds and high-quality utility and corporate bonds provide an excellent return. Long-term bonds, either interest-bearing or zero-interest bonds, do provide a consistent and guaranteed increased value in your plan.

What happens if the interest rate on long-term treasury bonds increases to 14 percent? First, it means that a bond paying a lower rate of interest (such as 10 percent) will drop in value. However, if you do not sell the bond, you will continue to receive the 10 percent per annum. Furthermore, the interest you receive on the bond each year and your annual contributions to your qualified retirement plan can now be invested at 14 percent per annum if you so choose. This means that you will continue to add to the assets in your plan. And if the interest rates decrease rather than increase, then you will have locked in a high rate of interest.

ADOPTING YOUR INVESTMENT STRATEGY

In the final analysis, you are the one who must adopt your investment strategy. You must choose those investments with which you will feel most comfortable. The information provided in Chapters 1 through 6 is intended to help you establish a foundation on which to build a strategy. Although the underlying principles of a sound investment strategy do not change, the strategy itself must be adapted to changes in your circumstances and changes in the economy.

Whether you acquire investments that are to be held in your name alone, such as gold, depreciable real property, growth stocks, or tax free bonds, or whether you acquire assets to be held in a qualified retirement plan, your strategy must be to seek value when you make the investments. If you are knowledgeable about a particular investment and not intent on "beating the market," you can usually acquire value.

Successful investors understand the importance of timing in adopting a successful investment strategy. William Shakespeare summed this up when he wrote:

There is a tide in the affairs of men,
Which, taken at the flood, leads on to fortune;
Omitted, all the voyage of their life
Is bound in shallows and in miseries.

Julius Caesar, IV, iii

Interlude

Unfortunately, many believe that only the wealthy, or at least those who have acquired assets, need to plan their estates. Isn't this why Part I on investment planning—the acquisition of assets—precedes Part II on estate planning? No, it is not. Estate planning is not necessarily something to be put off until one acquires assets.

True, the first step in estate planning is often reviewing your current assets—their value, how they were acquired, and how you presently hold title showing ownership. It also involves knowing how you want to dispose of these assets upon your death.

But the estate-planning process involves much more. Investment planning, tax planning, avoiding probate, appointing individuals or trust departments to manage your assets, acquiring life insurance to create an estate, and nominating an individual to make health-care decisions on your behalf are all part of the estate-planning process. The problems created by the death of a working spouse, the needs of orphaned children, and the care of elderly parents are as important estate-planning concerns as are minimizing taxes and distributing assets upon death.

Estate planning, like investment planning, requires your involvement. Its success depends upon the relationship between you and your estate-planning advisors. They must understand your objectives and your special areas of concern.

PART II

■

Estate Planning

Cujus est solum, ejus est usque ad coelum.
(Who owns the soil, owns it as far as heaven.)

Wills:
The Basic Document

Let's choose executors and talk of wills.
William Shakespeare, *Richard II*

While visiting a good friend, I commented on the beauty and attractiveness of his home and gardens. I was surprised when he said with a smile, "It's not really mine; I just use it while I'm here."

I later reflected on the truth of that unusual response. Although it may have been nothing more than a philosophical comment on the futility of spending too much of one's life worrying about "owning" or "acquiring" material wealth, his remark pointed out one very simple and obvious fact—we and our worldly possessions will one day come to a parting of the ways. There are no pockets in a shroud.

The single most important objective in estate planning—the distribution of your assets upon death to your beneficiaries in the manner you desire—is traditionally done by the preparation of your will.

A will is different from any other legal document that you sign. Your will is *ambulatory* until your death. This means simply that its legal consequences are not fixed until the event of your death.

USING AN ATTORNEY

You need not necessarily have an attorney prepare your will. In some states, you can write out your own will, provided it is entirely written, dated, and signed by you. You can also type your will. If it is signed by you and properly witnessed according to the laws of the state in which you reside, it will be valid. But is this a wise thing to do? Probably not. Drafting your own will is one of the best examples of being penny-wise and pound-foolish. There are several benefits in having an attorney prepare your will.

First, your will is the written expression of your intentions regarding the distribution of your assets upon death. Attorneys are simply more experienced at doing this kind of writing than are most laymen.

Second, wills do not necessarily control the distribution of all your assets upon death. The manner in which you hold title to your property will determine whether or not those assets are subject to distribution under your will. One of the responsibilities of an attorney in drafting your will is to make sure that your assets are properly titled so they pass as you intend them to.

Third, an attorney experienced in drafting wills may see problems or lost tax savings in your proposed plan of distribution and make suggestions that you might not have considered.

And last, even if your attorney tells you that yours is the simplest of situations and requires nothing more than a simple will that you could have done yourself, you will have the satisfaction of knowing that you have not left any unre-solved problems in the distribution of your assets upon death.

When you seek a lawyer to prepare your will, you want one who is experienced in preparing wills and planning

estates. Such a lawyer is often selected on the recommendation of friends and acquaintances who have had similar
work done and are satisfied with the results. Your accountant,
banker, insurance agent, stockbroker, as well as lawyers you
know through various organizations can also be helpful in
directing you to an experienced attorney.

If, in your initial conference, you do not feel comfortable
with the attorney, you find that you are unable to communicate, or you are not satisfied with the answers to your
questions, do not assume that it is because the preparation of
your will is a complicated matter that you cannot be expected
to understand. An inability to communicate with you may
indicate that the attorney does not understand your objectives
or lacks a commonsense approach to the solution of your
problems and therefore has difficulty in providing understandable explanations. Choose a lawyer in whom you have
total confidence. This is an important first step in the development of your estate plan.

KEEPING IT SIMPLE

Estate planning and wills are best kept simple. "Keep it
simple" is the common cry of all clients who struggle with
the frustration of attempting to comprehend lengthy documents filled with unintelligible legal jargon.

What is a simple will? It is a will in which you leave your
estate outright to your beneficiary(ies). For example, Calvin
Coolidge's entire will consisted of the following sentence: "I
leave my entire estate to my wife, Grace, and request that she
be appointed executrix without bond." If you leave your
household furniture, furnishings, jewelry, and clothing to one
or more individuals and then leave the balance of your estate

to be divided equally among ten beneficiaries, you have a simple will. A simple will is generally only three or four pages long, but can be longer, depending on the detail of the bequests. A simple will is easily understood and inexpensive to prepare. Most attorneys who prepare wills generally do so on an hourly rate for their time involved. Because a simple will usually does not require much time, the fees will usually be in the $100 to $200 range.

But a simple will can be costly when it requires a great deal of time on the part of your attorney. This can occur when you have a substantial number of bequests (recipients named in your will) and you take a lot of time and go through several drafts as you assemble your thoughts.

Even if your will is not costly, it is expensive when it does not meet your objectives. When bequests are left outright to beneficiaries to spend as they desire rather than in trust to be managed for them, or when a simple will results in much higher taxes being paid by your heirs because your will did not incorporate any tax planning, it is expensive indeed.

KEEPING A COMPLEX WILL UNDERSTANDABLE

A complex will is one in which bequests are not left outright to the beneficiaries but rather in a trust that will continue for some period of time. What if Calvin Coolidge's wife, Grace, had been mentally incapable of managing Calvin's estate, or if his only surviving son were a spendthrift, or if his deceased son had left children surviving him, or if he had wanted his estate to provide income for various family members with the balance being left to specified charities upon their deaths? Coolidge might be given high marks for having written a simple will, but not by his heirs.

A will should be complex when the situation requires something more than outright bequests. A complex will should still be understandable. It is your responsibility to understand both the reason for its complexity and how it will operate.

The following are some common situations that require a complex will.

Providing for Minor Children

When you have minor children, the will must provide for their custody (a guardian of the child). And because minors cannot hold title to property, the will must provide for someone to manage their assets (a guardian of the estate).

The guardian of a minor child may or may not be the same individual who manages the child's assets. Individuals who are excellent in raising children may have little or no experience in financial matters. Often parents with minor children have not had time to accumulate a substantial estate, and life insurance may be the principal asset. These proceeds and any other assets left to the children must be managed for them. For this reason, the guardian of a child's estate is often someone other than the guardian of the child. The guardian of the estate may even be a professional trustee such as the trust department of a bank.

It is common to create a trust (discussed in Chapter 10) to manage children's assets. What are the considerations in the establishment of such a trust? Let's assume that there are three children in the family, ages twelve, sixteen, and twenty-two. If the assets were divided equally among the three children, the twelve-year-old would take his third of the estate and be required to support and educate himself. The twenty-two-year-old, who had received her support and education out of the common assets of the family, will take her third and go out into the world. Thus, the twelve-year-old must pay out of his share of the estate what the oldest child received out of the family assets.

Because of this inequity, parents often want an arrangement that will treat the children in the same manner they would have been treated had the parents lived. And had this occurred, the support and education of each of the children would have come out of the family assets, with each child, in turn, receiving his or her share.

In order to approximate what would have been done if the parents had lived, the parents create a *family* or *pot* trust in their wills. The purpose of this trust is to keep the family's entire estate intact for the benefit of all the children. The trustee is given the power to use the income and principal for any of the children's support and education while taking into account their ages, their ability to be gainfully employed, and the size of the estate.

A family trust usually provides that when the youngest child attains some arbitrary age (such as twenty-one or twenty-three), the trust is divided into equal shares for the children, with each receiving an equal share of the balance. It is assumed that all of the children have by then been treated more or less equally and that they have all shared in the family's common assets.

When the trust is divided into these equal shares, a child's share can either be distributed outright to the child at that time, or each child's (or even a particular child's) share can continue to be managed by the trustee. The reason for continuing the trust is usually that the parents felt the child would still be too young to manage his or her assets and would be protected if the assets remain in trust and are managed for the child until he or she gains more experience. Even when this is done, the income and principal can be distributed to the child. But the child does not make the management decisions regarding the investment and reinvestment of the assets that are in the trust.

Clients often ask, at what age should this management responsibility be turned over to the child? In other words, when should the child's trust terminate? At the time the will is drawn, this question is often made even more difficult because the children are quite young and there is no way of knowing their future financial responsibility or capability of managing assets.

Some parents take the view that their assets should be distributed outright to their children when they reach majority. Others feel that the distribution of a child's estate should be done in stages, with the child receiving perhaps one-third of the principal at age twenty-five, one-third at age thirty, and the balance at age thirty-five. This staggered distribution of assets to a child is based on the theory that the child who foolishly spends the first distribution will have learned a valuable lesson. Furthermore, he or she will gain experience in financial matters and be less inclined to make the kinds of investment errors discussed in Part I of this book. Even children who are mature for their ages will learn more about managing and investing assets by experience than by reading a textbook.

There is a middle ground. You can provide that when a child reaches majority, he or she becomes a co-trustee of his or her trust. This means that the child is involved in the management decisions but cannot dispose of the assets unless the other trustee concurs. This will help the child gain experience while requiring a reliance on the judgment of a co-trustee.

There is no simple answer. It is a matter of your preference and the perceived ability of the child. The truth is that the age you usually select for the termination of the trust will relate more to *your* age than to any other single factor. The older you are, the more likely you are to delay the age of distribution.

There are some children who should never receive distribution of their trust principal and would be better off if it were managed for them for their entire lives. There are others who can handle their money at a very young age. It is said that when Joseph Kennedy, the patriarch of the Kennedy clan, set up trusts for his children, he provided that the principal would be distributed to them when they attained forty-five years of age. He thus had a son who was president of the United States, with the responsibility of establishing the economic policies that would guide the nation, and yet was still several years away from receiving distribution of his share of the family trust.

Tax Planning

Tax planning is discussed in greater detail in Chapter 13. Suffice it to say here that much of the tax planning that is done in wills is through the creation of trusts. Properly drafted trusts often provide income and estate-tax savings.

Second Marriages

In planning the estates of individuals who married more than once, we are often dealing with *his* children, *her* children, and *their* children. In addition, there are *his* assets, *her* assets, and *their* assets.

Suppose that when the wife dies, she wants her husband to have the benefit of her assets during his lifetime but wants to know that, upon his death, her assets will go to her children.

And suppose that he has the same desire for his assets. This situation is resolved by having a husband and wife each create a trust. If the husband dies, his assets will go into trust. The income will be distributed to his surviving spouse during her lifetime. Even the principal can be used by her if necessary for her support or to maintain her health. Generally, she has no other rights to the trust assets. Upon her death, the assets remaining in the trust will be distributed to his children. Likewise, the trust in the wife's will gives her husband the income and perhaps the same limited right to use principal. But upon his death, her trust assets will be distributed to her children.

Charitable Bequests

Some people want to leave all or part of their estates to a favorite charity. They may also want to ensure that members of their families have some benefit from those assets. These two objectives can be satisfied by leaving the assets in trust. The income will go to the family members for their lifetimes. Upon all their deaths, the remaining assets will be distributed to the charity.

If properly drafted, such a will can also substantially reduce the amount of income and death taxes that might otherwise be paid.

Disabled Persons

Disabled persons often receive federal and state aid because of their disabilities. The amount or extent of this assistance is often based on their other assets. If they receive any assets, the government aid may be reduced or even eliminated. Because of this, parents and other family members are often reluctant to leave assets outright to such individuals. Yet they often want to be sure that disabled family members are protected and that provision is made for their needs over and above any government assistance.

In order to do this, a trust can be established for the benefit of the disabled person. The trustee, usually a family member or someone who has personal interest in the disabled person, will be given the discretion to use as much of the trust income and principal as is necessary to provide these additional benefits to the disabled person. And because the disabled person—the beneficiary—does not own or control the assets in the trust, its existence will not jeopardize the benefits available under federal and state laws.

CHOOSING AN EXECUTOR

Your will names your executor. Your executor is responsible for gathering together your assets, determining your debts, including income taxes, and determining any death taxes that your estate may have to pay. Your executor is then charged with the responsibility of distributing the remaining assets as directed in your will.

Your executor may be any individual in whom you have trust and confidence. It may be someone who shares in your estate or someone, such as your attorney, who will assume these responsibilities. If there is no such individual, then the trust department of a bank may be appointed as executor.

An executor should be chosen on the basis of his or her ability to properly handle the responsibilities required in settling your estate. If your executor is an individual, particularly someone who is not a beneficiary of the estate, it must be someone who has the time to devote to what can be a very time-consuming and on occasion frustrating responsibility.

When an estate is to be distributed to a surviving spouse or to adult children, particularly when it is distributed outright rather than retained in trust, a family member usually acts as executor. The surviving spouse or child who will be receiving the estate is usually quite capable of assuming these duties with the help of an attorney.

Executors are entitled to be paid for their services. In most states the executor's fee is based on the value of the services rendered as determined by the probate court. In setting the fee, the court takes into account such factors as the time required, the complexity of the estate, and the expertise required by the executor in the performance of his or her duties. In some states, the executor is entitled to a *statutory* fee (a fee based on a percentage of the fair market value of the assets in the estate).

MATTERS RELATED TO WILLS

Funeral Arrangements and Anatomical Gifts

Funeral arrangements and arrangements to have various parts of your body donated for medical purposes should not be made in your will. Often a will is not read until it is far too late either to do anything about burial instructions or to see that parts of your body are donated to the organizations intended.

Family members who will be responsible for making funeral arrangements should be told of your desires or left instructions to be opened upon notification of death. Arrangements to have parts of your body given to organizations for transplant purposes or to be left for medical research should be made prior to death. Family members who are likely to survive your death should be aware of your desires.

Managing Assets in the Event of Incompetency

Your will disposes of your assets upon death. But what happens if you become incapable of managing your assets while you are alive? If you become incompetent, someone must have the authority to take control of your assets and do such things as writing checks and managing your assets. If nothing is done beforehand, a court-appointed conservator will have to assume these duties.

As a result of this problem, many states today have enacted legislation that allows you to authorize an individual of your choice to take over control of your assets in the event of your incompetency. You accomplish this by the execution of a power of attorney. Although powers of attorney used to terminate in the event of your incapacity, new legislation now provides that this will not occur. Thus, they are referred to as a *durable* power of attorney.

The Living Will and Durable Power of Attorney for Health Care

A common concern of clients is that they will be kept alive by various mechanical means when there is no likelihood of recovery and they are incapable of making any decision expressing their desires, and when they would neither want nor seek the full benefit of medical science under these cicumstances.

Because of this concern, the *living will* became popular. It was a directive to your physician not to prolong your life when there is no hope, not to subject you (and your loved ones) to the indignities, costs, and anguish of a prolonged period of dying. Questions arose about both the legal effect of a living will and whether it was really effective as a practical matter. As a result, many states authorized a *durable power of attorney for health care*. This is similar to the durable power of attorney for asset management previously discussed.

A durable power of attorney for health care allows you to give an individual the power to make all decisions relating to your medical treatment. This individual, who will know and follow your wishes, can make life-and-death decisions that are medically necessary if you are incapacitated. In those states that have enacted legislation authorizing the durable power of attorney for health care, the requirements of the statute must be followed and the durable-power-of-attorney-for-health-care form, rather than the living-will form, must be used.

MAKE SURE IT'S "YOUR WILL"

Today, more than ever before, virtually everyone gives you estate-planning advice. Unfortunately, much of the advice is limited to the objectives of the adviser and often fails to take into account your wishes and desires. The result is a will that does not accomplish your objectives—that does not accurately express your intentions for the distribution of your assets upon death.

The purpose of making a will is to leave your assets as you desire—not as your heirs might prefer, not as your attorney or accountant might recommend, and never with the sole objective of saving taxes or avoiding probate or any other objective that ignores your overall desires.

You must evaluate the advice you are given and put it (and its provider) in perspective. It is your responsibility to ensure that your will truly expresses your testamentary desires.

CHAPTER 8

Probate:
An Ugly Word

In the mid-1960s Norman F. Dacey's national best-seller, *How to Avoid Probate,* described the probate system as the enemy of the people—"a form of private taxation levied by the legal profession upon the rest of the population." For the last twenty years, avoiding probate has been a principal objective of many estate plans. What is probate? Why should it be avoided? Are there any advantages in having a probate proceeding?

WHAT IS PROBATE?

Technically, probate means the procedure by which your will is declared valid. More commonly, probate means the court proceeding by which your assets are upon death distributed pursuant to your will or, if you die without a will, are distributed pursuant to the laws of intestate succession (the laws in each state describing how assets are left to family members and relatives if you die without a will).

All assets that are your separate property are subject to probate. These would be assets that are registered in your name (such as an automobile, a piece of real property, or shares of stock), or assets that, although not registered in your name, are owned by you (such as furniture, works of art, or bearer bonds—bonds not registered in anyone's name that are considered owned by the holder of the bond).

When assets are held jointly with someone else (registered in your name and someone else's, such as a spouse, a child, or a friend), your interest in those assets may or may not be subject to probate. This depends on how title is held, such as community property, tenants in common, or joint tenants.

WHY AVOID PROBATE?

The most commonly stated objections to a probate proceeding are expense, delays, and publicity.

Attorneys' Fees and Other Costs

Both the personal representative and the attorney representing the personal representative are entitled to be compensated for their services in settling the estate. When Norman Dacey wrote *How to Avoid Probate,* most states based such compensation on a percentage of the value of the assets of the estate. The percentages for the attorney and executor varied depending on the size of the estate and on the state in which the probate occurred. Heirs objected to this method of determining the attorneys' compensation because it did not necessarily have any relationship to the work involved, the time committed, or the responsibility and expertise required in settling the estate.

As a result of the popularity of Mr. Dacey's book and the basic unfairness of this method of determining fees, most states have abolished the percentage or so-called *statutory fee.* Thus, the fee is based on the amount of time involved, the complexity of the estate, and the responsibility assumed by the attorney and the personal representative rather than on some arbitrary amount based only on a percentage of the value of the estate. Even in those states (such as California) that have retained the statutory fee, the personal representative may occasionally negotiate with the attorney a fee to be determined on some basis other than simply a percentage of the value of the estate.

The other probate costs are filing fees for the petition, publication costs, and the fees for the appraisers appointed by the court to determine the value of the assets. Usually these fees range from a few hundred dollars to a thousand dollars but rarely more than this amount.

Delays

Because the court administers a probate proceeding, probate requires time. For example, the appointment of the personal representative takes several weeks because all heirs and those having an interest in the estate must be notified and given an opportunity to raise any objections.

Once the personal representative is appointed, determining the nature and extent of the assets and the debts and taxes will require further time.

In most states creditors have from three to six months to file a claim. Because the personal representative cannot be sure what assets will be left in the estate after the payment of any such claims and debts, he or she cannot distribute the assets to the beneficiaries until the claim period has expired. Determining income-tax and death-tax liabilities may require further delays. Even when there is only one beneficiary of an estate and this person is also the personal representative, he or she has to comply with these technicalities. Understandably, this can be most frustrating.

Estates that are uncomplicated and are distributed outright to family members or other beneficiaries are usually distributed within one year of the date of death, with most such estates being distributed within six to nine months after the date of death. However, if the will is challenged or there are large claims pending against the estate or unsettled tax liabilities, the estate can be delayed for many years until these matters are settled.

Publicity

Because probate is a court proceeding, it is a matter of public record. Anyone can go to the county clerk's office and review your probate file. That file contains a list of assets owned at the time of death, a list of creditors, a copy of your will, and names and addresses of family members.

Notices of the filing of your will for probate are published in general-circulation newspapers. These notices inform everyone that a request has been made to admit your will to probate and sets forth the name of the individual you asked to have appointed as your personal representative. They also inform creditors that they must file their claims with the court. These publications, along with the public availability of the probate file itself, are of concern to many individuals.

ADVANTAGES TO PROBATE

There are some advantages to a probate proceeding. It offers an organized and established method of settling an estate. It provides a vehicle for gathering all the assets, determining all the debts and claims, and making distribution in accordance with the terms and provisions of one document—the will. It imposes on the personal representative the responsibility to ensure that distribution of assets to the heirs is only done after all legitimate claims and taxes have been determined and paid. In addition to an established forum for settling the estate, there are two other possible advantages: after a certain period, creditors' claims are invalid and taxes may be minimized.

Barring Creditors

As mentioned earlier, creditors of the decedent are given the opportunity to file their claims in the probate proceeding. The personal representative must then decide whether the claims are valid and, if so, provide for their payment before he or she distributes the assets.

If a creditor does not file a claim against the estate within the period allowed (usually three to six months from the date the probate is opened), these claims are barred and the assets are distributed to the beneficiaries. Thus, in the future, such creditors cannot collect their claims from the estate assets.

This can be of particular advantage when there is a possibility of claims arising after the decedent's death and after the period for filing claims in the estate has expired. For example, the estate of a professional person such as a doctor, lawyer, or accountant may have potential claims for malpractice committed during the decedent's lifetime. If such a claim should arise after the period of time for filing claims in the estate, the claimant is generally out of luck.

When assets are not subject to a probate proceeding but rather pass to individuals outside of probate, creditors may have four years or more after the decedent's death to pursue any claim they might have against the assets owned by the decedent at the time of death. Thus, probate may work in favor of the estate and its heirs.

Minimizing Income Taxes

A husband and wife will generally file a joint income-tax return because they will pay less in income taxes than if the husband filed a separate return on his income and the wife filed a separate return on her income.

When a spouse dies, the surviving spouse can file a joint return for the year in which death occurred. However, in the following year the surviving spouse must file as a single tax-payer. Thus, in the year after the spouse's death and in each of the following years, the surviving spouse will pay a much greater tax on the same amount of income received by the two before the death of the one spouse.

When there is a probate, the income on the deceased spouse's assets will generally be taxed to the estate as a separate taxpayer. This means that the income is not taxed to the surviving spouse. In the year following the year of death, the surviving spouse will pay the tax on his or her income and the decedent's estate will pay the tax on that income. Thus, the probate acts as an income-splitting device that has the effect of reducing the overall income-tax liability that the surviving spouse would otherwise pay.

Because of the probate estate, the surviving spouse will not pay tax on the income accumulated in the deceased's estate. This may be significant because the survivor will then be required to file as a single taxpayer and may therefore be in a much higher tax bracket than when the two were filing a joint return. Furthermore, when the income in the estate is later distributed to the survivor, it is not taxed because the tax has already been paid on it by the estate.

Thus, in those estates in which there is substantial income generated from assets subject to probate, the executor has the opportunity to engage in income-tax planning that can result in substantial saving. When this opportunity exists, it is necessary for the executor, the attorney, and the accountant for the estate to capitalize on it by planning very early in the probate proceeding.

Norman Dacey did not make the word *probate* ugly. It was made ugly because the process was not responsive to its intended purpose—the efficient and orderly windup and distribution of a decedent's estate. In his attack on the system, he struck a sensitive nerve.

Since the 1960s, every state has amended its laws pertaining to the probate of decedents' estates. The process has been streamlined and generally requires that far less information be filed with the court than was previously required. Furthermore, responsibility has been shifted to the personal representative, with less intervention by the probate court. Many states have also made it easier to avoid probate completely, especially when assets will pass to a surviving spouse or to adult children. For example, in California, if you want to pass assets outright to a spouse, these assets can be distributed without going through probate, even though they pass under your will.

Settling your estate by probate is an option you may take. There are others. Chapter 9 discusses various alternatives for the distribution of your assets.

Ways to Avoid Probate

*We [lawyers] were lulled into tolerating probate
procedures and tax systems that failed adequately
to serve the public. Alternative methods of transferring wealth, not using lawyers or court systems, have
developed and some of them work well.*
                Joe C. Foster, Jr., President of the
            American College of Probate Counsel

You can avoid probate in settling your estate, and there are
several good reasons for wanting to do so. This chapter
explores the various ways in which assets can pass to heirs
upon death other than under the terms and provisions of
your will, thus avoiding a probate proceeding.

THE REVOCABLE LIVING (INTERVIVOS) TRUST

The *revocable living trust* is a popular alternative to making a
will. Assets transferred to a living trust avoid probate. Because
its usage is so common, the revocable living trust is discussed
in detail in Chapter 11.

THE FORM OF TITLE TO YOUR ASSETS

How you hold title to your assets is a vital consideration.
Your estate planner reviews the form of title to your assets to
determine whether it is consistent with the tax and estate-

planning objectives for the disposition of your assets upon death. When property is registered in your name alone ("Mary Smith, individually" or "Mary Smith, a married woman, as her sole and separate property"), then upon death, the property is subject to probate. It will be distributed pursuant to the provisions of your will. If you die without a will, such property will be distributed by the laws of intestate succession (the laws that determine to whom your assets go when you die without a will).

If title to your assets is held jointly (in your name and the name of at least one other individual), then whether such assets are subject to probate (and thus disposition under your will) will depend on the exact form of title. The forms of joint ownership are joint tenancy, tenancy in common, tenancy by the entirety, and community property.

Joint Tenancy

In *joint tenancy,* each joint tenant owns an equal interest in the property. Any two or more individuals can take title to assets as joint tenants. A husband and wife who reside in a community-property state can also hold title as joint tenants.

Joint tenancy carries with it a *right of survivorship.* This means that when one joint tenant dies, the other or others become the sole owner or owners of the asset. A decedent's interest in assets held in joint tenancy does *not* pass under the terms and provisions of his will but rather passes to the surviving joint tenants.

For example, assume a husband and wife hold their bank accounts and real properties in both their names as joint tenants. The husband's will leaves his one-half interest in these assets to his children by a prior marriage. Upon the death of the husband, his interest in these assets is not subject to disposition under his will and the assets are not subject to probate. Contrary to the provisions in his will, they will pass automatically by right of survivorship to his surviving spouse.

Assume a single person places her bank accounts in her name and that of her housekeeper as joint tenants. This is done so that the housekeeper can draw on these accounts in the event of her employer's incapacity. However, under her will, the woman leaves these bank accounts to her niece. Upon her death, these bank accounts are automatically passed to the housekeeper because she is the surviving joint tenant.

Tenancy in Common

Tenancy in common differs in two important respects from joint tenancy. First, tenants in common do not necessarily have equal interests in the property, as do joint tenants. For example, you and a friend may hold title to a piece of property as tenants in common, and the friend may own a 20 percent interest in the property and you may own an 80 percent interest.

The other principal difference between this form of joint ownership and joint tenancy is that tenancy in common does *not* carry with it a right of survivorship. Thus, in the two examples I cited in my discussion of joint tenancy, the husband's interest in joint assets held as tenants in common would not go to his surviving spouse; rather, his one-half interest would go under his will to his children by the prior marriage. And the single person's interest in the bank accounts would not go to the housekeeper, but to the decedent's niece. In other words, a decedent's interest in assets held as tenants in common will be a part of his or her probate estate and distributed by the will or by the laws of intestate succession.

Tenancy by the Entirety

Tenancy by the entirety is a form of holding title only between a husband and wife who reside in a separate-property state. A separate-property state is one that has not adopted community property.

Tenancy by the entirety also carries with it a right of survivorship. As with joint tenancy, any such assets will pass automatically to the surviving spouse and will not be probated.

Community Property

Community property is a form of holding title only between a husband and wife who reside in a community-property state. Community-property states are those states that have adopted this form of holding title to property (Arizona, California, Idaho, Louisiana, Nevada, New Mexico, Texas, and Washington).

The community-property laws are different in each state. But generally each spouse's half-share in the community property will pass under his or her will. Thus, it forms a part of that spouse's probate estate. However, some community-property states, such as California and Washington, also permit community property to pass to the surviving spouse without probate. This can occur if community property is left outright to the surviving spouse under a will or if the parties sign an agreement that they want their community property to pass outright to each other. Then when one dies, his or her interest in the community assets will pass directly to the surviving spouse and will not be subject to probate.

Advantages and Disadvantages

One form of ownership is not necessarily better than another. Whether assets should be in your name alone or in your name and a spouse's name or some other individual as joint owners will depend on the answer to a number of questions, including the following:

Are you single or married?

If you are married, do you intend to leave your interest in your assets outright to your spouse or do you intend for your interest in your assets to be distributed in some other manner, such as a trust for the benefit of your spouse and children?

Will there be estate taxes payable upon your death? Upon your spouse's death?

Do you have assets that have appreciated substantially in value?

Do you live in a community-property state?

How you answer these and other questions will determine the best form of title for your assets. For example, for many married couples, holding title to their property as joint tenants is the best choice. Upon the death of either of them, joint tenancy assets will pass outright to the surviving spouse with a minimum of delay, costs, and fees. There is no probate proceeding, and the surviving spouse will immediately take control of these assets.

But joint tenancy is not for every married couple. If the husband does not intend for his assets to go outright to his wife upon his death, but rather prepares a will in which his half of their joint assets is to go into a trust for her benefit during her lifetime and ultimately for the benefit of their children, then for them joint tenancy is the wrong form of holding title to their property. If they hold title to their assets as joint tenants, these assets will pass outright to the survivor. This is not what they want. They want the interest of the first to die to be added to the trust established under his or her will. Thus, the joint tenancy form of holding title to their property is inconsistent with their intentions.

If the estate of a married couple is so large that they are concerned about estate taxes, or if their estate has assets that have appreciated substantially in value, then these considerations may dictate against holding title to their assets as joint tenants. The joint-tenancy form of holding title may be inconsistent with the tax planning required when there are estate-tax and income-tax problems.

Joint Tenancy as a Will Substitute

Because assets held by individuals as joint tenants pass upon death to the surviving joint tenant and are not subject to probate, the joint tenancy is often thought of as a will substitute.

Whenever you place title to your property in your name and the name of anyone else as a joint owner, for whatever reason, you must understand that this form of holding title to your assets indicates who the owners of that property are. This is one of the principal differences between a will and joint tenancy. When you sign a will, you don't transfer any interest in your assets; you only state your wishes for the disposition of these assets upon your death. But when you create a joint tenancy, you transfer ownership at the time joint tenancy goes into effect.

For example, if a mother takes her stocks, bonds, and home and places them in joint tenancy with her son, upon her death, these assets will pass automatically to him and will not be subject to probate. However, at the moment she transfers the title into his name as a joint tenant, he immediately acquires a one-half ownership interest in these assets. This means that his approval is required to sell these assets. And it means that his creditors may attach his interest in these assets as payment for his debts. If the assets produce income, the Internal Revenue Service will consider that half the income belongs to the son because he owns half the assets.

Thus, if you create a joint tenancy to avoid probate or to accomplish any other estate-planning objectives, you must take into account all the legal implications of transferring title to your assets into someone else's name as joint owner.

LIFE INSURANCE

When you acquire life insurance, you enter into a contract with the insurance company. That contract provides that you will pay premiums and that when you die, the insurance company will pay a fixed amount to a designated beneficiary. The primary beneficiary is your first choice to receive the proceeds. A secondary beneficiary is the one who will receive the proceeds if the primary beneficiary is deceased.

These amounts are paid to the beneficiary directly. They are not part of your probate estate unless you name your estate or the executor under your will as the beneficiary.

The trustee of either a *testamentary* (created by will) or a *living* trust can be named as either the primary or secondary beneficiary of the insurance proceeds. If you name the trustee as beneficiary, then the insurance proceeds will be paid to the trustee and will be subject to the terms of the trust agreement. These proceeds will not be probated. Also, if you purchase an annuity from an insurance company, the annuity payments will be made to the designated beneficiary and will not be part of your probate estate unless expressly made payable to your estate.

Insurance is a good example (but only one of many) of an asset that is subject to federal estate tax even though it is not subject to probate. Life-insurance proceeds paid on the life of a decedent who owned the policy at the time of death are taxable for federal estate-tax purposes. Even so, depending upon the total value of the decedent's estate and who the beneficiaries are (for example, a spouse or a charity), there may not be any federal estate tax payable.

PAYMENTS UNDER AN IRA, KEOGH ACCOUNT, AND CORPORATE PENSION AND PROFIT-SHARING PLAN

Your interest in a retirement account or plan is treated in a manner similar to life insurance. You designate the beneficiary, and these amounts will be paid directly to the named beneficiary or beneficiaries without being part of your probate estate.

BANK TRUST ACCOUNTS

There is a form of holding title that only applies to bank or savings-and-loan-association accounts. It is referred to as a *Totten trust.* This is an account that you open in your name as trustee for the benefit of some other individual, for example, John Doe as trustee for the benefit of Harry Smith. During John Doe's lifetime, he alone controls the account. He can withdraw the entire amount, thus revoking the trust, or make partial withdrawals at any time. During John Doe's lifetime, Harry Smith has no rights to the account. However, upon John Doe's death, any balance in that account will be distributed to Harry Smith, the beneficiary. Such an account is not part of John Doe's probate estate. Because the Totten trust is a form of holding limited to financial institutions, it cannot be used in taking title to stocks, bonds, real property, or other assets.

Arranging your assets to avoid probate is quite easy. Successful estate planning, however, depends far more on what you accomplish than on what you avoid. First, you want to carry out your wishes. Doing so in a way that minimizes costs, expenses, taxes, and legal entanglements is a secondary consideration.

You Need a Trust

Put not your trust in money but put your money in trust.
Oliver Wendell Holmes

Trusts are used extensively in estate planning because their flexibility allows the trustor to carry out a variety of estate-planning objectives, ranging from minimizing taxes to prudently managing assets. The trustor's estate-planning objectives determine whether the trust is a *living* trust or a *testamentary* trust (whether the trust is revocable or irrevocable during the trustor's lifetime).

The word *trust* describes a legal relationship that is created when persons transfer the titles to their assets to trustees with the intention that the trustees manage these assets for the benefit of individuals or charities. The person creating the trust is known as the *trustor, settlor, donor,* or *creator.* The individuals or charities receiving the benefits of a trust are called *beneficiaries.*

The terms of a trust are almost always contained in a written agreement, which describes both how the trustee is to manage the assets and how the income and principal are to be distributed to the beneficiaries. The trustee may be an individual, the trustor, two or more individuals, or a professional (*corporate*) trustee, such as the trust department of a bank. When there is more than one trustee, they act as co-trustees, each sharing responsibility for managing and administering the trust estate. A trustor will sometimes choose to have a corporate trustee along with one or more individuals as co-trustees.

CREATING A TRUST

There are two ways to create a trust. The first is to create the trust during your lifetime. A trust created in this manner is called a *living* or *intervivos* trust. Under a living trust, the trustor's assets are transferred to the trustee during the trustor's lifetime. This is commonly referred to as *funding* the trust. Although a living trust comes into existence at the time it is signed by the trustor, it requires that the title to your assets be transferred to it at that time. The trustee then manages the assets transferred to the trust in accordance with the trustor's intentions as set forth in the trust agreement.

The second method of creating a trust is to provide in your will that your assets be left in trust. Because this type of trust is created in your will and therefore does not come into existence until after your death, it is called a *testamentary* trust. A testamentary trust is established when the assets are distributed from the decedent's estate to the trustee. Thus, the creation of a testamentary trust requires that there be a probate proceeding because the trust is created pursuant to the provisions of your will.

HOW TRUSTS OPERATE

When you create a trust, you essentially do two things:

1. You name the individual, corporate trustee, or combination of both who will be responsible for the management of the trust assets.
2. You describe the individuals and charities who are to receive the income and principal of the trust both during its existence and when it terminates.

A common question asked by clients about the creation of a trust is, "Doesn't a trust tie up my assets?" The answer depends on what you mean by "tying up" your assets. When you create a trust, it may be *revocable* or *irrevocable*. Obviously, if it is revocable, your assets are not tied up because you can revoke the trust at any time and have the assets transferred to it returned to you.

But what if the trust is irrevocable? For example, you create a trust for your children that will become irrevocable at the time of your death. Although your children cannot revoke the trust, this does not mean that the trustee cannot pay income or principal to them. The trustee can make distributions to them to the extent the trust allows such payments to be made.

The trustee's major responsibility is to manage the assets of the trust. For example, if cash is transferred to the trust, it is the trustee's responsibility to invest that cash. The trustee can purchase common stocks, bonds, or real property. And any assets acquired by the trustee with that cash will remain subject to the trust. The trustee must also decide whether assets are to be held or sold, and if sold, how the proceeds are to be reinvested.

The trustee's responsibility for managing trust assets is governed by provisions in the trust agreement. In most trust agreements the trustee is given broad latitude in the choice of investments. If the provisions in a trust are not clear or are absent, all states have laws that require a trustee to act as a "reasonably prudent person" in managing the trust assets. In exercising this power of management, the trustee must do so in a manner that protects the trust assets for the intended beneficiaries.

The trustor in creating the trust can impose any restrictions he or she desires on how the assets will be managed. The trustor can, for example, provide that the trustee cannot acquire common stocks. Or the trustor can direct the trustee to only invest assets in bank accounts guaranteed by the federal government. The trustee will then be restricted to such investments.

Trustees are *fiduciaries* (persons who manage trust assets for the benefit of the beneficiaries). As trustees they are held to a high standard of accountability. (It is not uncommon for beneficiaries to sue trustees for falling below this standard.) Trustees should therefore be conservative in investing the trust assets.

In creating a trust, a trustor can impose restrictions on how the assets are to be managed. By limiting the trustee's discretion, the trustor can in a sense "tie up" the trust assets. For example, during the depression of the 1930s, many individuals lost confidence in the stock market. During this period they created trusts that often severely restricted the trustee's authority to invest and reinvest the trust proceeds. In some instances the trustee could invest only in government bonds or corporate bonds of the highest quality. These restrictions imposed on the trustee were unfortunate, particularly in trusts that continued for many years, because such investments produced a very low return.

Restricting the investment powers of the trustee is generally unwise. Trustees should be selected on their ability to manage the trust assets. Restricting their powers may have unfortunate consequences if the restrictions prevent the trustees from capitalizing on economic changes unanticipated by the trustor.

In addition to the management responsibility, a trustee is also responsible for the disposition of the income and principal of the trust to the beneficiaries. In trust law the term *principal* refers to the assets transferred to the trust and any growth or increase in the value of these assets. *Income* refers to the return, such as interest, dividends, or rents. Thus, beneficiaries may receive income and principal during the time that the trust is in existence. The beneficiaries (unless they are also trustees) will not, however, be making the management decisions, such as which assets are to be sold, which are to be held, and how proceeds are to be reinvested.

THE USE OF TRUSTS IN ESTATE PLANNING

Trusts are commonly used in estate planning because of the many objectives they can help planners accomplish, including the following: management of assets, estate-tax savings, avoidance of probate, controlling the distribution of income and principal at some future date, income-tax planning, and avoidance of conservatorship or guardianship.

Asset Management

Imagine that you are married and have always managed the family investments. And you are concerned that, in the event of your death, your spouse will be incapable of managing these assets; or you are making provisions for your children but are concerned about their spending tendencies; or you are elderly and no longer wish to spend your time managing your assets. Whatever the situation, a desire to have someone else take over the responsibility of managing your assets is a perfectly sound reason for creating a trust.

When you create a trust it should be revocable. If you are not satisfied with the arrangement, you can revoke it and the assets will be returned to you. You can also restrict the trustee's power to make any investment or reinvestment of the trust assets without your prior approval.

. When you give assets to some individual, such as a child or a spouse, but do not feel that this person is capable of managing the assets, you are creating a trust for management reasons. The beneficiary of this type of trust should not be given the power to revoke it.

Estate-Tax Saving

Trusts are used to minimize estate taxes. When property is left outright to a spouse or to another beneficiary, those assets will be taxed at the time of his or her death. If assets are not left outright but rather are left in trust, with a spouse or parent receiving only the income from the trust, then such assets will not be taxed upon the death of that spouse or parent.

A trust allows the beneficiaries to have the economic benefits (the use of the income from the assets) without the disadvantages of having those same assets included in their estates for either probate or estate-tax purposes. Minimizing estate taxes is discussed further in Chapter 13.

Avoiding Probate

Creating a revocable living trust to avoid probate is discussed in Chapter 11.

Controlling the Future Disposition of Assets

Individuals often want their estates to be distributed to a particular person or a particular charity but also want to provide income to various other beneficiaries. For example, suppose you want to provide for your new wife but, upon her death, want your assets distributed to your three children by a prior marriage or to a charity of your choice.

The trust allows you to provide income to your wife during her lifetime and, upon her death, to have your assets distributed to your children or to charity in accordance with your desires.

Income-Tax Planning

Trusts are often created to minimize income taxes. Suppose you want to use the income from your assets to support your parents or your children. If these assets are transferred to an irrevocable trust and the trustee is directed to pay the income to your parents or children, then the income will not be taxed to you; it will be taxed to them. Because they are usually in a lower income-tax bracket, there will be less tax paid on this income.

Sometimes the trustee is given the right to distribute the income to the beneficiary, accumulate the income in the trust, or sprinkle the income in varying amounts among several beneficiaries. This, too, may result in a lower overall income tax on the income generated by the trust assets.

Avoiding Conservatorship or Guardianship

If you transfer your assets to a trust during your lifetime and later become incompetent, the trustee will continue to manage these assets pursuant to the terms of the trust agreement. This will avoid the expense of having a court-appointed guardian or conservator assume this responsibility.

Each trust is unique, tailored to meet the needs of a particular situation. The terms of the trust will vary, depending on the reasons for its creation. When used wisely, trusts can help minimize taxes and protect beneficiaries. The use of a trust often provides the most sensible distribution of your estate.

CHAPTER 11

The Revocable Living Trust

The magic key is the intervivos or living trust,
a financial bridge from one generation to another.
Norman F. Dacey

The revocable living trust, sometimes called the revocable intervivos trust, is often recommended by accountants, trust officers, financial planners, attorneys, and financial writers as a will substitute—a method of distributing your assets upon death without probate. It is created for two principal reasons: management of assets and avoidance of probate.

When trustors want an individual or a financial institution to manage their assets during their lifetimes, they transfer title to these assets to a revocable living trust, naming that individual or institution as trustee. The trustee will then invest and reinvest the assets, collect the income, and make distributions to the trustor in accordance with the trust provisions. The trustor can revoke or amend the trust at any time if dissatisfied. When the trustor dies, the trustee will make distribution of the trust assets in accordance with the provisions of the trust and without probate.

When a revocable living trust is created solely to avoid probate, the trustor does not intend to give up management of the assets during his or her lifetime. The trust acts primarily as a will substitute effective upon the trustor's death. In this case, the person who was managing the assets before the creation of the revocable trust (the trustor) normally will be the same person managing the assets once they are transferred to the trust (the trustee). Furthermore, when trustors create trusts solely to avoid probate, they intend to receive the benefits of the trusts during their lifetimes. Therefore, trustors are also beneficiaries of the trusts during their lifetimes.

THE REVOCABLE LIVING TRUST VERSUS PROBATE

In a revocable living trust, when the trustor dies, the assets transferred to the revocable living trust will be distributed pursuant to its terms rather than pursuant to the terms of the trustor's will.

Under the living trust, the alternate trustee named in the trust is responsible for the administration of the trust assets when the trustor dies or becomes incapacitated.

The individuals and charities who are to receive the income and principal on the death of the trustor are considered beneficiaries of the trust at the time it is established even though they will not realize the benefits of the trust until the death of the trustor. Their rights under the trust agreement are simply postponed until that future time, just as they are under a will.

Earlier chapters discussed the reasons commonly given for the avoidance of probate—fees and costs, delays, and publicity. The revocable living trust helps to reduce or eliminate these problems largely because no court-supervised probate is needed.

Fees and Other Costs

The trustee of the revocable living trust has the responsibility for settling the estate of the trustor and distributing the assets.

The fees paid to a trustee for services are not necessarily based upon a percentage of the estate, nor are they set by a court. They are negotiated with the beneficiaries. Thus, fees may be charged on a time basis, a percentage basis, or even a combination of the two.

Particularly where the distributions are made outright to the beneficiaries and there are no tax or other complications in the estate, time-based attorney's fees may be minimal compared to the fees for a probate estate. The higher fees in a probate estate are caused by a combination of the statutory fee based on a percentage of the estate and the involvement of the court.

Delays

The trust agreement can provide that, upon the death of the trustor, the trust will terminate and the assets will be distributed to the beneficiaries. Thus, an advantage of the revocable living trust is that both the income and the principal of the trust are immediately available to the beneficiaries.

This can be particularly advantageous in those situations in which the estate is to be distributed outright to beneficiaries, such as adult children. The alternate trustee can distribute the assets without any unreasonable delay and does not have to wait for court approval, as would be the case with probate.

Publicity

There is no publicity involved in the administration or distribution of assets from a revocable living trust. The payment of taxes and claims and the distribution of assets are handled by the trustee without any court involvement. There is no file opened at the county clerk's office. There is no public record of the proceeding. The only parties who ordinarily have any

knowledge of the trust are the trustee and the trust beneficiaries.

Avoidance of Guardianship or Conservatorship

An advantage of creating a revocable living trust is that it can
simplify management of the trustor's assets should he or she
become incapacitated, as by advanced age, illness, or acci-
dent. If you have created a revocable living trust and become
incapacitated, the alternate trustee named in the trust agreement will take over the management of the trust assets. There
will be no need to have a court appoint a guardian or
conservator of your estate to take over these management
responsibilities.

Even if you have not created a revocable living trust, you
can avoid the necessity of a court-appointed guardian or conservator by executing a durable power of attorney for asset
management (see Chapter 7). This will give the individual
named in the instrument the right to assume the management
of assets in the event of your incapacity. It eliminates the
need for any court involvement.

ESTATE-TAX SAVING

You may have read or been told that a revocable living trust
will avoid probate and can save death taxes. This may have
given the erroneous impression that because the revocable
living trust avoids probate, you therefore obtain an estate-tax
saving. You do not obtain an estate-tax saving *because* you
avoid probate. Assets transferred to a revocable living trust
are subject to federal estate taxes upon the death of the
trustor. For federal estate-tax purposes, assets in the trust are
treated as though owned by the trustor.

Under certain circumstances, an artfully drawn revocable living trust can minimize or eliminate estate taxes. However, an artfully drawn will can, under those same circumstances, minimize or eliminate the same amount of estate tax. It is *not* true that a revocable living trust, regardless of how skillfully drawn, can save a greater amount of estate tax than can be saved by the identical provisions in a will. Similarly, a will, regardless of how skillfully drawn, cannot save more estate taxes than a revocable living trust.

So whether your estate is settled by your alternate trustee named in your revocable living trust (without probate) or by your executor named in your will (with probate), the estate-tax consequences will be the same.

OTHER IMPORTANT CONSIDERATIONS

The following are some considerations that you should review prior to transferring your assets to a revocable living trust.

Payment of Debts and Taxes

The alternate trustee of a revocable living trust will be responsible for settling the trustor's estate and distributing the assets upon the death of the trustor. In other words, the trustee must perform the same duties that an executor would perform under a will. The principal difference is that these duties, when performed by a trustee rather than an executor, are not subject to the approval of a court and can therefore be done without adhering to the legal requirements and delays of a probate proceeding.

As stated earlier, one of the advantages of the living trust is that assets can be transferred and income and principal can be immediately distributed to the intended beneficiaries upon the death of the trustor.

But what about the debts of the trustor that remain unpaid at death? The trustee must pay funeral expenses, unpaid bills, income taxes, estate taxes, and other liabilities out of the trust assets. If the trustee distributed the assets to beneficiaries who then refused to contribute to the payment of these debts, costs, and taxes, the trustee would be personally liable for them. The relative informality of settling the trust can cause these items to be overlooked. Although the trustee could require the beneficiaries to reimburse him or her for these expenses, this could be time-consuming, expensive, and perhaps even fruitless if the beneficiaries no longer had the assets. Thus, the alternate trustee, unless also the sole beneficiary of the trust, is well advised to delay the distribution of any trust assets until satisfied that sufficient assets exist to make these required payments.

Extended Time for Creditors to File Claims

Another consideration concerning the living trust is that there is no procedure to limit the time for creditors to file claims, as there is in a probate proceeding. Ordinarily, this time period for filing a claim is relatively short (three to six months). When there is no probate, creditors have a much longer time to pursue a claim against assets owned by the decedent. Thus, the alternate trustee cannot distribute the assets with the same assurance that all the debts have either been paid or provided for.

This can be important if the decedent was a professional or in a business where there is a possibility of claims arising at some time in the future. For example, a doctor or lawyer who does not have malpractice insurance may have a situation in which claims could arise long after death.

When there is a probate and assets are distributed pursuant to a court order, the heirs are protected from creditors who did not timely file their claims in the probate proceeding.

Cost of Comparisons

Most attorneys involved in estate planning charge on an hourly basis for their services. This means that the greater the time and effort, the higher the cost. Attorneys may also vary their hourly rates based on the complexity of the matter involved. Generally, the cost of establishing a revocable living trust is greater than that for a will because of the additional time and complications that sometimes arise in attempting to transfer the title of various assets to the revocable living trust.

A revocable living trust is not effective until assets are transferred to it. The trustor's assets are transferred from the name of the trustor to the name of the trustee so the trustee will hold title subject to the terms of the trust agreement. Transfer of assets is not required in a will because the will only becomes operative upon death. The will only operates on those assets held by an individual at the time of death.

When the assets being transferred to a living trust are real property, bank accounts, or stocks and bonds, transferring title to the trustee is not particularly difficult. However, where the trustor has interests in limited partnerships, notes secured by real property, or extensive holdings, the transfer of title to the trustee can be time-consuming and expensive.

Income-Tax Saving

As discussed in Chapter 8, there may be income-tax advantages in having a probate estate. However, an executor's opportunity to minimize income taxes in settling an estate is usually not available to the trustee of a revocable living trust.

Assets Not Subject to Probate

Many assets are not subject to probate and will pass directly to heirs. For example, a joint-tenancy property passes outright to the surviving joint tenant, and retirement plans, insurance and annuity proceeds, and bank-trustee accounts are paid directly to named beneficiaries and are generally not subject to probate. If probate is not required for the distribution of such assets, it may not be necessary to create the trust for this purpose.

Creating a Revocable Living Trust Solely to Avoid Probate

If you reside in a state where the probate system is cumbersome and expensive with high fixed fees paid to attorneys and executors, then you should seriously consider establishing a revocable living trust. If you want your estate settled without a court proceeding, the saving in probate costs in settling your estate can easily be 50 percent or more.

The balance clearly tips toward the revocable living trust when, in addition to avoiding probate, there are lifetime benefits to be gained from its creation. When you want someone else to manage your assets during your lifetime (in which case you will not be the trustee) or you are concerned about your mental capacity or being influenced by other individuals, and you want to ensure that your assets are protected, then the revocable living trust will provide the desired security.

There is also an advantage in knowing that once your assets are transferred to the trustee under a revocable living trust, then upon your death, they will be distributed pursuant to the terms and provisions of the trust. This avoids the confusion that is often caused by individuals who sign wills but hold their assets jointly with other people and in a manner in which they will not be distributed under the wills. For example, placing assets in your name and that of someone else as joint tenants, as previously discussed, will mean that they are not subject to your will. This title problem is avoided when title to your assets is transferred to your revocable living trust.

The reasons given for creating a revocable living trust are often not sound. One investment advisor in his book on real estate recommended the creation of a living trust because the Rockefellers, the Kennedys, and the superrich do it. This is not a valid reason for doing so.

Furthermore, the advantages of the revocable living trust are often exaggerated. Financial planners, attempting to gain your confidence, often make it sound as though creating a living trust will resolve all your estate problems.

Exaggerating the benefits of a revocable living trust may leave the heirs with the false impression that all the estate problems are resolved. When they later discover that the living trust does not solve these problems, they are left frustrated and unprepared to deal with them. One excellent true example can be seen in the case of Mrs. Jones. Her husband had created a revocable living trust in order to avoid probate and make things easier for her in settling his estate. The principal asset in the trust was a piece of real property that did not produce any income. Though it had a high value, it was difficult to sell or lease because of a depressed real estate market. As a result, the trust did not have sufficient cash to pay the death taxes. Eventually the real property was sold, the death taxes were paid, and Mrs. Jones had sufficient income for her support. However, this took more than a year to accomplish. When the sale was finally concluded, Mrs. Jones said that if her husband had had any idea how the revocable trust had worked, "he would roll over in his grave."

There was nothing improper in using the living trust to avoid probate. It was effective in accomplishing its purpose. Unfortunately, it could not (and did not) eliminate the basic problems that confronted Mrs. Jones upon her husband's death. These and other problems will often arise after death whether assets are held by the trustee of a revocable living trust or by the executor under a decedent's will. The principal purposes of the estate-planning process are to anticipate these potential problems and, to the extent possible, to deal with them. To pretend that they do not exist or that there is a legal document that can make them disappear is simply to indulge in wishful thinking.

The revocable living trust is an important tool in the estate-planning arsenal. It can accomplish many estate-planning objectives. However, these objectives and the problems that arise in settling an estate must be approached realistically and with common sense.

CHAPTER 12

Choosing a Corporate Trustee

When you create a trust, one of the most important considerations is choosing a trustee. The trustee is responsible for the
investment and reinvestment of the trust assets, the collection
and distribution of income, and the payment of expenses.
The choice of a trustee or co-trustees will be based on two
principal considerations: the reason for creating the trust and
the availability of qualified candidates.

THE CHOICE OF A TRUSTEE AND THE REASON FOR CREATING THE TRUST

Trusts are created for a variety of reasons, including avoiding
probate, saving taxes, and managing assets. The principal
reasons for creating the trust will bear significantly on the
choice of a trustee. For example, if a husband and wife create
a revocable living trust for the sole purpose of avoiding probate, the trust is created to act as a will substitute. They want
to retain control over the management of the assets transferred
to the trust during their lifetimes. Therefore, they would act

as co-trustees. In the event of the death or incapacity of either, the survivor would act as the sole trustee.

But what if they create a trust because they are concerned that, in the event of the husband's death, the assets will be distributed to minor children or to beneficiaries who, in their opinion, are not capable of managing the trust assets? Here they must consider as trustee someone in whom they have confidence. They can name one or more individuals, a corporate trustee such as a trust company, the trust department of a bank, or co-trustees that include both an individual and a corporate trustee.

Selecting individuals to act as trustees can be extremely difficult. Those persons who have the time to devote to managing the trust assets often are not knowledgeable in making investment decisions. And individuals who are capable of making the investment decisions are often so busy they cannot commit the required time. Accordingly, a corporate trustee is often selected to act either as the sole trustee or as a co-trustee with one or more individuals. When you choose a corporate trustee, pay particular attention to the relationship between the trustee and the beneficiary.

THE CORPORATE TRUSTEE AND THE BENEFICIARIES

Many times one spouse does not take any interest in the family investments because the other spouse has assumed that responsibility. The spouse responsible for the investments may have made arrangements for a corporate trustee to take over that responsibility. For example, if a husband is responsible for investing the family's assets, he might name a corporate trustee to carry on the investment responsibility in the event of his death.

However, the surviving spouse, who had no reason during her husband's lifetime to be involved in the investment of her assets because he handled them, may now have a much stronger motive to be involved because these decisions will have a direct effect on both her standard of living and her security. At the time the husband draws his will (or living trust), he has no way of knowing how his wife will react to this responsibility in the event of his death.

In these situations it is often advisable to consider naming a corporate trustee and the surviving spouse as co-trustees. Even though the surviving spouse may not be interested in being actively involved in making the investments and may be quite willing to leave this responsibility entirely to the corporate trustee, the surviving spouse will necessarily be involved in the investment policies of the trust as a co-trustee.

Whether or not a surviving spouse is a trustee, it is generally recommended that he or she (unless a hopeless spendthrift) be given one of several powers over the corporate trustee (for example, the power to veto any proposed investment or reinvestment by the corporate trustee). This would require the corporate trustee to communicate with the beneficiary prior to taking any such action. Thus, the surviving spouse will always be aware of what is happening in the trust. Unless there is a strong reason for not doing so, giving a surviving spouse a veto power will avoid the frustration that can occur when the beneficiary has no opportunity to give any input into the actions of the corporate trustee.

If you do not want to give a surviving spouse or other beneficiary the power to veto any proposed investment, you may want to give this power to a third person. For example, you may require the corporate trustee to obtain the approval of an independent investment advisor or investment firm in whom you have confidence before investing trust assets.

Independent investment firms and advisors are often unwilling to be trustees but are agreeable to this more limited role.

Another power that you may want to include is the right of the surviving spouse to replace the corporate trustee with another corporate trustee of his or her choosing. When the surviving spouse has this power, it rarely needs to be exercised because the corporate trustee is more conscious of the importance of maintaining a good relationship with the beneficiaries. It is like the relationship between the spectators and the cross-eyed javelin thrower—although he didn't have much chance of winning the gold medal, he certainly held their attention.

As you will see from some of the situations discussed later in this chapter, a positive relationship between the corporate trustee and the beneficiaries is often the key to the success of the trust.

What Corporate Trustees Say About Themselves

Enter the offices of any trust company or the trust department of any bank, and you will find brochures that describe the benefits of a trust and the reasons you should use the services of that particular corporate trustee. The following are some statements taken from one such brochure:

> The primary purpose of a trust is to provide for the dynamic management of your assets. The trustee must deal with a wide variety of business and financial considerations. We will administer your trust in a skillful and professional manner.

> Naming us as your trustee will provide security, convenience, and flexibility in the distribution of income and principal among your beneficiaries.

Our staff includes people who are experienced in all phases of trust administration. We understand the importance of maintaining a personal relationship with the beneficiaries and an understanding of their present and future needs. We work hard at carrying out our responsibilities in both the business and personal side of a successful trust administration.

Because we maintain a close and friendly relationship with the beneficiaries, you can be assured that each beneficiary will derive the maximum benefits from a trust created for his or her benefit.

WHAT THE COURTS AND SOME BENEFICIARIES SAY ABOUT CORPORATE TRUSTEES

Trustees, individual or corporate, have responsibilities and duties to the trust beneficiaries. When they do not perform these duties in a prudent manner, the beneficiaries may sue them, as in the following three cases.

The Stone Heirs

In 1946 J. T. Stone purchased a corner of real property in downtown Seattle, Washington. He transferred the property to a trust with the Pacific Bank, now First Interstate Bank, as trustee. Mr. Stone established what is known as a *generation skipping trust,* which provided that the income would go to his children (the second generation) for as long as they lived and that upon their deaths, the trust assets would pass to his grandchildren (the third generation).

In 1978, without the knowledge of the Stone heirs, the bank sold the property. It did this in spite of a letter from the beneficiaries informing the bank that the property was not to be sold without their prior knowledge. Under the trust agreement, the bank had the legal right to exercise its own judgment and discretion in decisions relating to the investment and reinvestment of the trust assets.

The Stone heirs sued the bank for breach of its fiduciary responsibility to them in the manner in which the sale was held and in not informing them of the pending sale. The bank contended that the sale was conducted in good faith, with honest judgment, and that under the trust instrument, it had absolutely no duty to inform the beneficiaries of any such sale. The bank stated that its decision to sell or not sell any of the trust assets was its sole right and responsibility as trustee.

After a lengthy trial in the Superior Court of the State of Washington, the judge ruled in favor of the bank. This court accepted the bank's argument that it did not have to ask the beneficiaries for permission to dispose of the trust property and therefore had no liability. The court added insult to injury by allowing the bank to pay its attorney's fees incurred during this litigation out of the trust assets.

However, the Supreme Court of the State of Washington reversed the lower-court decision and found that the bank had breached its fiduciary duty of good faith, loyalty, and integrity owed to the beneficiaries. It also determined that the attorney's fees and costs were incorrectly charged to the trust. The supreme court found that the bank's conduct in the management of the Stone trust was "an egregious breach of fiduciary duty and defies the course of conduct any reasonable person would take, much less a prudent investor."

The Anderson Heirs

The second case involves T. Albert Anderson, who died on May 3, 1982, naming the Bank of America as executor and trustee under his will. The principal asset in his estate was a thirteen-thousand-acre ranch in Glenn County, California. The beneficiaries of his estate were his surviving spouse and two children.

The bank had authority to sell the ranch and did so. The heirs filed suit, claiming that the sale was not properly handled. After a twelve-day trial, the bank was found to be grossly negligent, incompetent, and imprudent for the manner in which it handled the entire transaction. The court stated, "The bank had failed to give the slightest degree of skill or expertise in the discharge of its duty as executor." It awarded the heirs damages in excess of $1,500,000.

The Gump Heirs

Another case involves the Wells Fargo Bank, which in 1969 was appointed trustee of a trust established under the will of Abraham L. Gump.

In 1978 the income beneficiaries of the Gump trust sued the bank, alleging breach of its duty to them. They sought actual damages and asked that the bank be charged with *punitive* damages. (Punitive damages are awarded when a court wishes to punish a defendant for its conduct.)

The court found that the bank had failed to provide information about the sale and purchase of securities despite repeated requests that such information be provided, that it threatened to charge additional trustee's fees for making trust property productive, and that it threatened to charge additional fees for correspondence if the beneficiaries did not cease inquiry about the bank's handling of the trust's assets.

After a lengthy trial, a judgment was rendered for the beneficiaries in the amount of $23,000 damages. The court also found that the bank's conduct during the course of its administration of the trust reflected malice, oppression, and fraud. The court awarded the beneficiaries $1 million in punitive damages, holding that the bank's actions were unconscionable. The judge who granted this award said the bank's officers lost sight of the fact that they were supposed to be working for the beneficiaries rather than for the bank and that they seemed to think it was their money.

These three cases are not examples of why you should never use a corporate trustee. There are many individuals who would not enjoy the standard of living that they do if it were not for a corporate trustee managing their assets. Furthermore, there are many trusts in which the relationship between the corporate trustees and the beneficiaries is excellent.

What these cases illustrate is that both corporate and individual trustees have a legal responsibility and duty not only in the way they manage the trust assets but also in the way they maintain the relationship with the beneficiaries. It is the beneficiaries—the ones for whom the trust is created—who are the true owners of the trust assets. Trustees are fiduciaries who control and manage assets that they do not own. They have a duty to act in a responsible and prudent manner.

SOME REASONS FOR CONSIDERING A CORPORATE TRUSTEE

Some individuals name corporate trustees because they have great confidence in them. Others name corporate trustees because they do not know any individuals who are qualified to assume the duties of a trustee. Whatever the reason, there are advantages to using a corporate trustee.

Corporate trustees have substantial professional investment experience. They often rely on the services and expertise of outside financial advisors.

Corporate trustees are impartial in making trust investments. Unlike financial planners and other investment advisors, they do not receive commissions based on the purchase and sale of trust assets.

Corporate trustees are conservative. The majority of their investments are in stocks and bonds of good quality. They also have the capability of managing real estate and other kinds of assets.

Corporate trustees provide a continuity of management. You cannot be sure how long an individual will be able to carry out the duties, but when you name a corporate trustee, you know that individuals who are experienced in the management of assets will be making the investment decisions.

Corporate trustees will take possession of assets, collect the income, keep records, and pay taxes. Many individuals are quite willing to pay to be relieved of these burdens.

If a corporate trustee makes a mistake or one of its employees embezzles trust assets, the trust beneficiaries will not suffer any loss as a result of the trustee's negligent or criminal conduct. A corporate trustee is a trustee with "deep pockets" and has financial responsibility.

There may also be tax advantages to using a corporate trustee that may not be available when a member of the family who is a beneficiary of the trust is also a trustee.

Whatever your feelings about a corporate trustee, there are situations in which naming one as the sole trustee or as a co-trustee is the only sensible choice. When a trust is created because the beneficiaries are spendthrifts (that is, they would recklessly spend any assets left to them), because children are minors or incapacitated, or because there is concern that beneficiaries will be influenced by others (such as their spouses), then clearly a corporate trustee should be considered. The job of a trustee in these circumstances can be both thankless and threatening. To name a brother, sister, or some other relative as the trustee for a member of the family can bear heavily on the personal relationship.

CORPORATE-TRUSTEE FEES

A trustee, corporate or individual, is entitled to be paid for services rendered in the management of the trust estate. Individuals, particularly those who are beneficiaries or family members, often waive their fees. However, if they charge a fee, it will generally be based upon a comparable fee charged by a corporate trustee for the same services. A corporate trustee will usually charge an annual fee based on a percentage of the fair market value of the assets being managed.

If the corporate trustee does not have management responsibilities but simply retains custody of the trust assets, collects the income, and transfers this income to the beneficiaries, its charges will be in the range of 0.5 percent for these custodial services. Thus, if the value of the assets is $500,000, the bank would charge $2,500 per year for acting as custodian.

If the corporate trustee performs these duties but is also responsible for investing and reinvesting the trust assets, it will generally charge annual fees of 1 to 1.5 percent of the fair market value, depending on the nature of the trust assets.

If the assets are stocks and bonds, the charge will be in the 1 percent range. If the trust includes real property and requires care of the property and its leasing, then the trustee's charge is usually 1.5 percent or more. Thus, if the value of the trust assets is $500,000, the bank's annual fee would be in the range of $5,000 to $8,000 per year.

In addition to these fees, corporate trustees often charge additional fees where other services are required, such as negotiating for the sale of real property or representing the trust in a tax audit by the federal government.

Can you negotiate trustees' fees? Yes, you can, particularly when a corporate trustee is managing a revocable living trust. However, when the trustor dies and the trust becomes irrevocable, the trustees often increase their management fees because they will assume additional duties.

When a corporate trustee assumes the responsibility for settling the trustor's estate, it normally charges, in addition to its management fees, additional fees based on the value of its services in settling the estate.

If there is a co-trustee named to serve with the bank, the bank will charge a higher-percentage fee than if it had the sole responsibility for administering the trust. At first, this would appear contradictory. Why should a corporate trustee charge more when, as a co-trustee, it has a shared responsibility (and liability) rather than the sole responsibility? Corporate trustees feel that if there is a co-trustee with whom they must communicate in making investment decisions, it will take more time than if they had the sole right to make these same decisions. Because a corporate trustee's fees are based on a percentage of the fair market value of the trust and not on the amount of time it spends on managing trust assets, a corporate trustee makes the greatest profit when it manages the largest amount of assets in the least amount of time. Since a co-trustee usually increases the amount of time a corporate trustee must spend in managing the trust assets, it feels justified in charging additional fees by increasing its percentage.

An individual co-trustee is in a much stronger position to negotiate fees when he or she has the power to replace the corporate trustee with another corporate trustee who might be more willing to negotiate its charges.

ADVANTAGES TO USING A CORPORATE TRUSTEE

Trustees may be family members, personal friends, business acquaintances, or family advisors such as the family lawyer, accountant, or other financial advisor.

In choosing family members, you may be putting them in an awkward position when they are required to manage assets and perhaps even exercise their discretion in distributing income and principal to various relatives. But when family members are reasonably intelligent and have at least an average amount of common sense, they, along with your accountant, family advisor, trusted employee, or lawyer, may be made co-trustees or nominated as advisors to the co-trustees.

Here you create an arrangement very similar to the board of directors of a corporation. The board is responsible for making policy decisions. Thus, including family members and trusted advisors assures everyone's input into making investment decisions. Control of your assets by your family and family advisors is often preferable to dealing with a trust-department employee who may have little or no knowledge of the business, investments, and needs of the various family members.

There can be advantages in using a corporate trustee, and in some instances it is the best choice. However, when a corporate trustee is named as either trustee or co-trustee, the continuing relationship between the corporate trustee and the beneficiaries must be given careful consideration.

CHAPTER 13

Ways to Avoid Death Taxes

There are two kinds of death taxes. One is imposed by the federal government and is called the federal estate tax. The other is imposed by the state governments and generally is called a state inheritance tax. During the past ten years, there have been a number of changes in our tax laws, none of which have been more dramatic than in the areas of the federal estate tax and the state inheritance taxes. As a result, the federal estate tax, the state inheritance tax, or both have been eliminated or substantially reduced in many estates. This elimination or reduction was brought about in three principal ways:

1. The federal estate-tax exemption was increased from $60,000 in 1976 to $500,000 in 1986 and $600,000 in 1987 and thereafter.
2. All assets left to a surviving spouse are completely exempt from any federal estate tax.
3. State inheritance taxes were repealed in many states as a result of the "taxpayer revolt" of the late 1970s.

If you want to plan your estate wisely, you should be aware of the federal estate tax, how it operates, and some common approaches for reducing or eliminating it.

DETERMINING IF YOUR ESTATE HAS A FEDERAL ESTATE-TAX PROBLEM

The federal estate tax is a tax on your right to transfer property at the time of your death. The first step in computing the amount of the tax is to determine the value of your gross estate. If your gross estate is less than the estate-tax exemption at the time of your death, there is no estate tax.

If your gross estate is more than the amount of the exemption, you may take various deductions to arrive at the taxable estate. These deductions include debts outstanding at the date of death, liens against assets included in the gross estate (such as mortgages, real-property taxes, and expenses of administering the estate, such as attorney's, executor's, and trustee's fees). There is also a further deduction for property that passes to a surviving spouse. This is called the marital deduction. When assets are distributed to charitable organizations, there may also be a charitable deduction for such distribution. If, after you take these deductions into account, the taxable estate is less than the amount of the exemption at the time of death, there will be no federal estate tax.

Determining the Value of Your Gross Estate

Your gross estate includes all assets owned by you at the time of your death. Assets such as your home, stocks and bonds, bank accounts, automobiles, business interests, and personal effects are all part of your gross estate. Your gross estate may also include some assets that you may not realize will be a part of your estate, such as the following.

Life Insurance

Life-insurance proceeds on your life are included in your gross estate if you *own* the policy or if your estate is beneficiary. You own the insurance policy when you retain any of the *incidents of ownership.* For example, if you retain the right to change the beneficiary or to borrow against the policy, then the insurance on your. life will be your asset and included in the value of your gross estate. If the ownership of the policy (the incidents of ownership) are owned by your children or some other beneficiary, then the proceeds will not be included in your gross estate because you are not considered to be the owner of that policy.

IRA, Keogh, and Corporate Retirement Plans

The value of your interest in any of these retirement plans is included in your estate at the fair market value at the time of your death. The assets in these plans are beginning to constitute a significant share of estates.

Assets Held As Joint Tenants

If you and another hold property as joint tenants, your gross estate includes a proportionate value of the property based on your original contribution. For example, if you purchased a home but placed it in your and your son's names as joint tenants, then upon your death, 100 percent of the value of the home would be included in your gross estate because you contributed 100 percent of the consideration for the purchase of that home. But if your son dies, no part of the value of the home would be included in his estate because he contributed nothing toward its purchase.

Revocable Living Trusts

As mentioned in Chapter 11, your gross estate also includes the value of any assets transferred to a revocable living trust. Even though the revocable living trust avoids probate, the assets transferred to it are subject to federal estate tax in the estate of the donor.

Valuing Assets in Determining Your Gross Estate

The assets included in your gross estate are valued at their *fair market value*. Fair market value is the price for which the assets would be sold on the open market.

Transfers Between Spouses—The Marital Deduction

One of the most dramatic changes made in the federal estate-tax laws in 1981 was the adoption of the *unlimited marital deduction*. This means that if an estate, regardless of its size, is left outright to a surviving spouse or is in a trust that meets certain requirements, there is no federal estate tax. For example, if a husband leaves his wife his entire estate consisting of $2 million in assets, there cannot be any federal estate tax on his estate at the time of his death because the entire amount qualifies for the marital deduction.

If assets are not left outright to a surviving spouse, but are left in trust with the surviving spouse receiving only the income from the trust, these assets may qualify for the unlimited marital deduction provided the trust meets various requirements under the Internal Revenue Code. This is called a *qualified terminable interest trust* or *Q-TIP trust*.

The purpose of a Q-TIP trust is to allow a spouse to leave his or her estate in trust with the income going to the surviving spouse and to direct to whom the trust is distributed upon the death of the surviving spouse. For example, assume that a husband has two children by a prior marriage. In the event of his death, he wants to provide for his wife but also wants to be assured that, upon her death, his assets will be distributed to his children by his prior marriage. With a Q-TIP trust, he can give his wife the income and direct that the assets be distributed to his children upon her death.

Under this kind of trust, the personal representative of his estate can elect, in effect, not to pay any federal estate tax at the time of his death but rather to have any tax deferred until the time of the wife's death. This is the *Q-TIP election*.

The marital deduction often does not eliminate the federal estate tax (although this is what it does in the husband's estate), but rather simply defers that tax because these assets (including any increase in their value) will be included in the wife's estate for federal estate-tax purposes. In other words, the federal estate taxes are deferred until the assets pass to the children, at which time they will be paid. It eliminates the hardship that previously arose upon the death of a husband or wife when the surviving spouse was required to pay a substantial tax.

The Charitable Deduction

Assets transferred to a charity may qualify for the charitable deduction even if they are not left outright to the charity but are transferred to a trust that pays the income to some individual beneficiary for some period of time before the assets are distributed to the charity.

THE AMOUNT OF YOUR ESTATE TAX

The estate-tax rate begins at 37 percent on those amounts that are subject to tax after the exemption and the deductions described above. The transfer tax is progressive. This means that the rate of taxation increases as the value of the estate increases. It ranges from 37 percent to 55 percent. This 55 percent rate begins on estates that exceed approximately $3 million.

How to Minimize or Eliminate Death Taxes

When the gross estate exceeds the amount of the estate-tax exemption, tax planning becomes important. There are a number of ways in which the death taxes may be either minimized or eliminated:

1. You can create a *bypass* trust in your will or living trust.
2. You can make gifts during your lifetime.
3. You can take advantage of the marital or charitable deductions or both.
4. You can have the executor or trustee of your estate make various estate-tax elections, such as Q-TIP, that will have the effect of reducing the amount of estate tax or deferring the time of its payment.

Creating a Bypass Trust

Assume that a husband and wife have a $1 million estate of which each owns half. They intend to provide for the survivor during his or her lifetime, and then upon the death of the survivor, to leave their estate outright to their two adult children.

If the husband dies first and leaves his $500,000 to his wife, there will be no estate tax. (The gross estate is less than the amount of the exemption. Furthermore, the entire amount qualifies for the unlimited marital deduction.) However, upon the death of the wife, there probably will be an estate tax because the wife's estate will be larger than the exemption and a marital deduction might not be available.

How can the surviving spouse have the economic benefits (the right to use income and principal) of the estate of the first to die and yet not have those assets added to his or her estate upon death? The solution is to create a bypass trust. In a bypass trust the husband will not leave his $500,000 outright to his wife; rather, he will leave it in a trust for her benefit. His wife will receive the income from this trust until she dies. Furthermore, she can be the sole trustee of the trust, and as trustee she can have the right to use the principal for her support and maintenance. However, when she dies, the trust will terminate and the husband's $500,000 will go to their children. Because the husband's $500,000 was not left outright to his wife but rather in a trust, when she dies, it will not be subject to federal estate tax. Therefore, by creating a trust, the husband's $500,000 "bypasses" his wife's estate for estate-tax purposes. And because her assets ($500,000) are less than the exemption amount, there will be no estate tax on her own assets when she dies.

If the wife dies before her husband, then she makes the same provision for him and her $500,000 will not be included in his gross estate for federal estate-tax purposes.

As previously mentioned, after 1986 each decedent's estate will have an exemption of $600,000. Any amount up to the exemption amount that is left in a bypass trust will not be taxed on the death of the first to die or on the death of the second. It will pass to the children or other ultimate beneficiaries tax-free. This means that by simply creating a bypass trust, a husband and wife will each be able to leave $600,000 to their children or other beneficiaries, a total of $1,200,000 by both parents, free of any federal estate tax.

Making Gifts During Your Lifetime

The Annual Exclusion

You can give up to $10,000 each year to each of as many individuals as you desire, and you will not be required either to pay any federal gift tax or to file a federal gift-tax return. This $10,000 exclusion from gift taxes is called the *annual exclusion*. It applies whether or not the donee is related to you. You can give $10,000 to a total stranger, and that gift comes within the annual exclusion.

The annual exclusion is based on the gifts made to various persons during a calendar year. For example, during one calendar year you can give $10,000 to each of your three children, $10,000 to each of their spouses, and $10,000 to each of your seven grandchildren. And although you will have given away $130,000, you will not pay any gift tax and you will not file a gift-tax return. Further, none of the recipients will have to pay any gift tax on the amount you give them. If you are married, your spouse can do the same. Furthermore, in January of the following year you can give these donees another $130,000 without any gift-tax consequences.

Giving More Than the Annual Exclusion

It is true that gifts given during your lifetime can reduce your estate taxes at death. But such gifts cause you to lose control of the assets that are transferred. So before making a large gift, you must decide that: (1) you can afford to give it and not jeopardize your own security and (2) you are willing to give up control. Having made these decisions, you should examine the death-tax benefits of making substantial gifts.

Gifts during your lifetime that exceed the $10,000 annual exclusion are to that extent added to assets you own at death to determine the amount of death tax that must be paid.

The following example illustrates this point: Assume that in 1986 you give $110,000 to a child. Of this amount, $10,000 qualifies for the annual exclusion. The $100,000 will reduce the amount of exemption that would otherwise be available at the time of your death, but you will not pay any tax at the time of the transfer.

If you die after 1986 with $550,000 of assets, your heirs will have an estate tax to pay based upon $650,000 of assets—the

$550,000 you owned at death plus $100,000 of the $110,000 gift you made in 1986. Of course, the full $600,000 exemption is available, so taxes will actually be paid on $50,000 ($650,000 less the $600,000 exemption).

If the amount of gifts in excess of the annual exclusion is added back to the gross estate at the time of death, what are the advantages of making the $110,000 gift in 1986? First, the income that the $110,000 would generate and be added to your estate will be earned directly by your heirs. Second, if the value of the $110,000 gift goes up, then this appreciation has escaped taxation at the time of your death. This appreciation may be especially important for gifts of stock, business interests, and real property.

Gifting Your Interest in Life Insurance Policies

Life insurance is included in your gross estate and thus is subject to federal estate tax. However, if you transfer the incidents of ownership to your children or to an irrevocable trust for your spouse and children within three years of death or if they own the incidents of ownership at the time the insurance is acquired, then the insurance proceeds will not be subject to federal estate tax.

Because insurance proceeds are necessary to provide for the support and maintenance of the family or to pay death taxes, it is unfortunate when the proceeds themselves cause additional tax. It is relatively easy to avoid death taxes on life insurance, but doing so requires that you give particular care to the designated *owner* (not the beneficiary) of the policy.

The Marital and Charitable Deductions

Gifting Between Spouses

As previously mentioned, you may leave any amount to your spouse without incurring federal estate tax. You may also give, during your lifetime, assets to your spouse without incurring any federal gift tax. Giving assets to a spouse is particularly advantageous when the spouse has few or no assets of his or her own. By giving him or her sufficient assets up to the exemption that would be applied to that estate, you may make these transfers to future heirs without ever having the assets taxed.

Making Charitable Gifts

Assets transferred to qualified charities either during your lifetime or at death will be exempt from gift and estate taxes. Furthermore, if you transfer them during your lifetime, income-tax advantages may also accrue to you.

Determining the Basis of Property

There are tax differences to a beneficiary who acquires assets by gift rather than by inheritance at the time of death. The rule you should keep in mind when making substantial gifts of assets during your lifetime relates to the *basis* of property in the hands of the donee. Basis of property is the amount that is used in determining gain or loss on the sale of the property. The basis of property is usually your cost.

Assume, for example, that you purchased one hundred shares of common stock for $10,000 and over the years these shares increased in value to $50,000. Your basis, that is, your cost, is $10,000. If you sold this stock during your lifetime, you would have a capital gain of $40,000. This gain is computed by subtracting your basis of $10,000 from the sale proceeds of $50,000.

What happens to the basis if you give these shares to your son? When you give assets during your lifetime, the donee will take your basis. Thus, if you transferred all these shares to your son, he would take your basis of $10,000.

What happens to the basis if you hold onto these shares and then leave them to your son upon your death? Because these shares are included in your gross estate, they receive a *new* basis at that time. And this new basis is the fair market value of these shares at the time of your death. These shares will receive a new basis even though there may be no federal estate tax to be paid at the time of your death.

Thus, if these shares are included in your gross estate at a value of $50,000, and if your son sold these shares for $50,000, he would have neither gain nor loss because this asset received a new basis at the time of your death.

There is an important difference in how basis of an asset is determined by a donee (donor's cost) and by the beneficiary of an estate (value at decedent's death). This difference is an important consideration in planning your estate and choosing which assets to transfer during your lifetime and which assets to hold and pass to your beneficiaries at the time of death.

Thus, if assets such as common stock or real property have appreciated substantially in value, a beneficiary would be far better off receiving them by inheritance (thus receiving a new basis) than by gift (thus retaining the donor's lower basis).

POSTMORTEM TAX PLANNING

Postmortem tax planning is the planning that takes place after your death that reduces either the income taxes or estate taxes that would otherwise be paid. The personal representative of your estate, whether it is the executor under your will or a trustee under your living trust, may be able to make a number of elections that, if properly exercised, may reduce or eliminate both income and estate taxes in the settlement of your estate.

In order to take advantage of these elections, your personal representative should consider them as a first order of business in settling your estate. This planning begins as soon as the personal representative becomes knowledgeable about the assets of your estate. Two important postmortem estate-planning considerations are special-use value and deferred payment of federal estate taxes.

Special-Use Value

As previously mentioned, the value of assets included in the gross estate is their fair market value. When an asset is valued at its fair market value, it is valued at its highest and best use (what someone would be willing to pay for this asset were it put on the market for sale).

When an estate includes real property used as part of a family business or a farming operation, that real property may have a value far in excess of its value when used in the business or farming operation. For example, if you have a farm that has value as potential subdivision property, the value of the real property is probably far greater than its value as a farm. If the real property is used as part of a family business or farming operation and meets various legal requirements, the estate administrator may elect to have that real property valued at far less than its fair market value. This election can reduce the value of the real property by as much as $750,000.

The purpose of this provision was to make it easier for family businesses and family farms to be left to heirs. In many instances in the past, death taxes were often so large that the family farm or business had to be sold simply to pay them. This provision was intended to provide relief from that situation.

Deferred Payment of Federal Estate Taxes

The federal estate tax is payable nine months after date of death. However, where the decedent's estate includes an interest in a farm or a closely held business, the law may allow an extension of up to fourteen years in which to pay the tax.

Under this law the executor or trustor, as the case may be, may pay interest for only four years. Thereafter the estate tax is paid in ten equal annual installments. The interest on the first $1 million of such estate tax caused by the property is 4 percent per annum.

A FINAL WORD ON TAX PLANNING

Tax planning might be compared to taking medicine. Although a particular medicine may achieve a spectacular immediate result, its benefits must often be weighed against its potential adverse side effects.

Most tax planning has side effects. For example, we can say with certainty that if you give your assets away, you will reduce any potential estate tax liability at the time of your death. It is difficult, however, to estimate how long you will live, how well your assets will hold up in a changing economy, and what your future needs will be. It is also often difficult to predict the impact of making gifts upon donees. Many times the desired result is not achieved, such as the education or advancement of the donee. Instead, the gifts may simply be squandered on frivolous pursuits.

Creation of the bypass trust is probably the best example of a tax plan that often eliminates any estate-tax liability while having very few, if any, adverse side effects. This is true because the surviving spouse will have essentially the same economic benefits from the trust assets that he or she would have had if the assets had been left outright rather than in a trust. Leaving the assets in trust may provide heirs a substantial estate-tax saving.

I once met with a client who was considering making gifts to her children. It was a program recommended by her accountant as one method of saving taxes. It would also have made her dependent upon her children. After discussing the matter thoroughly, she decided against making the transfers. She said, "I believe my accountant was more concerned about what happens when I die than what happens if I live."

Tax planning is an important part of estate planning. But good tax planning is always done within the context and framework of the estate plan, and any promised benefits must be balanced against any potential nontax disadvantages.

CHAPTER 14

Choosing Professional Advisors

Let the counsel of thine own heart stand
For no man is more faithful unto thee than it.
Rudyard Kipling

In making investments and in planning your estate, you will necessarily rely on the knowledge and advice of attorneys, accountants, and investment advisors. Your choice will bear heavily on the ultimate success or failure of your planning.

As discussed in previous chapters, bad planning can be the result of relying on advisors who lack knowledge and experience or who, although knowledgeable and experienced, are more interested in selling and promoting an investment product than in serving your best interest.

Bad planning can also be the result of relying on the advice of "experts" and "specialists." Experts' knowledge is no guarantee that their recommendations are consistent with your objectives. Furthermore, investment and estate-planning specialists can become too enamored of their craft. Attorneys and accountants who have reputations as "tax experts" often overemphasize tax considerations and underemphasize the nontax aspects of investment and estate planning. They can be guilty of overplanning and may develop plans that are inflexible and fail to take into account the unforeseeable changes that inevitably occur in the economy and in personal relationships.

THE RELATIONSHIP BETWEEN
CLIENTS AND ADVISORS

When you choose to rely on the recommendations of any advisor, you assume that he or she is "loyal" to you—that the advice you are given is in your best interest. All professional advisors, whether attorneys, accountants, or investment advisors, are compensated for their services. The question is not how or how much they are paid, but whether you are getting value for these services.

How do you know whether these services are worth what you are paying? To answer this question you must understand the relationship between you—the client—and your advisors. The advice you receive, be it an investment of your money in a tax shelter or the creation of a trust, will require a course of conduct on your part. Your advisor's responsibility is to recommend approaches that complement the objectives you have defined. You must decide whether or not to proceed.

Walter T. Fisher (an attorney) in his book, *What Every Lawyer Knows,* describes the dependent relationship of a lawyer and a client by comparing it to the nondependent relationship of a doctor and a patient. What he says about the lawyer-client relationship would also apply to financial or estate-planning advisors and their clients. Fisher states,

> The doctor has a relatively free hand in his treatment of disease. It is this freedom which constitutes the major difference between doctors and lawyers, namely, that the patient does not generally participate much in the numerous decisions as to how his illness is to be treated. But the client characteristically participates with the lawyer in numerous decisions, large and small, as to what must be done to carry out each ultimate purpose. . . . It is notoriously undesirable to turn any expert loose with power to act for you unless you understand as well as you can what he is doing for you.

You may delegate but never abdicate your responsibility in the areas of financial and estate planning.

PROFESSIONAL ADVISORS
AND WHAT THEY DO FOR YOU

Attorneys, accountants, trust officers, stockbrokers, sellers of insurance, financial planners, and pension consultants are among those who provide investment and estate-planning advice. What do they do and what are their responsibilities to you? Following is a discussion of their duties, first as commonly understood by you—the client, and second as viewed by the respective professionals.

The Client's View

Lawyers

Lawyers provide knowledge of the law. They give advice and warnings on what is legally permissible, draft legal documents, give tax opinions, negotiate contracts, and represent clients in court and before governmental boards and commissions. Lawyers draft your will or living trust. They may write letters on behalf of clients who feel that a letter from a lawyer will have greater impact than ones they write. Although clients seek the assistance of lawyers in planning and settling estates, they do not think of lawyers as investment advisors.

Accountants

Accountants keep financial records and prepare tax returns. They also make recommendations on how to minimize income-tax liability. If returns are audited, accountants represent their clients before the Internal Revenue Service. Accountants may also provide business and investment advice with particular emphasis on those actions that will minimize clients' taxes.

Investment Advisors

Stockbrokers sell stocks and bonds as well as a wide variety of other investments such as tax shelters and mutual funds.

Insurance men and women sell life insurance, annuity policies, and often give estate-planning advice. If you do not have an attorney or accountant, they will provide you with recommendations on which ones are knowledgeable in the investment and estate-planning fields.

Trust officers employed by bank trust departments manage assets and administer trusts and estates. As administrators they collect income, pay expenses, and make distributions to beneficiaries. They also provide distributions of income and principal to beneficiaries and assume investment responsibilities for stocks, bonds, real property, and money market investments.

Financial planners provide a wide variety of services that range from preparing budgets to providing investment, legal, and estate-planning advice. They put on numerous "free" seminars directed primarily toward mutual funds and tax-shelter-type investments.

The Professional Advisor's View

Lawyers

Lawyers draft legal documents and provide legal advice. But they feel that their responsibility is greater than simply carrying out preconceived ideas that clients bring to them. Working with clients, lawyers often act as "devil's advocates," making sure the clients know and have considered all the available choices.

Lawyers place their highest value on their independence. They do not view their relationships with clients as ones in which they simply do what they are told. They make suggestions based on their experience and on what they deem to be in a client's best interest. They consider the entire problem rather than simply taking the next step.

Lawyers often have the responsibility to coordinate the activities of those involved in investment and estate planning. If you view the various investment and estate-planning individuals who serve you as a team with your best interest as its objective, then your lawyer considers himself or herself to be the captain.

Accountants

Accountants see themselves playing a much broader role than that of preparing financial records and tax returns. Because clients often insist that accountants be aggressive in making recommendations that will reduce their tax liabilities, accountants have frequently been involved in recommending various tax-sheltered investments.

Accountants, like attorneys, consider themselves to be independent and objective in the advice they give. For these services they usually charge on an hourly basis and do not receive any benefit from the sale of an investment product.

Accountants see themselves particularly suited to coordinate clients' investment and estate-planning activities because they are familiar with clients' day-to-day business dealings. They are knowledgeable about estate planning and estate settlement. Although the advice given by accountants and attorneys often overlaps, it is in the client's interest that there be a good working relationship between these two advisors.

Like attorneys, accountants view themselves as the most qualified to be the team captain.

Investment Advisors

The advent of financial planners has changed dramatically the role of investment advisors. There is no longer such a thing as a stockbroker, an insurance person, a mutual funds salesperson. You can buy life insurance and annuities through a stockbroker. You can buy mutual funds and tax-sheltered investments through an insurance person. Even stockbrokers refer to themselves as "financial consultants" or some other title clearly indicating that they do more than simply sell and buy stocks and bonds.

Financial planners view themselves as not only capable of recommending virtually any conceivable kind of investment you might desire, but also of making the recommendations pertaining to your overall investment and estate plan. Financial planners will often direct a client to an attorney but provide specific instructions as to his or her legal duties. Financial planners not only see themselves as the team captain coordinating the activities of the other professionals involved; they often want broad control over clients' investment decisions.

Even trust companies and banks are involved in the sale and purchase of stocks and bonds and the preparation of financial plans. Although banks advertise that the only place you can find a banker is in a bank, it is also true that you find stockbrokers and financial planners in banks, just as you find savings and checking accounts (money market funds) in brokerage firms.

GAUGING YOUR ADVISOR'S INDEPENDENCE

Just because professional advisors are loyal to your best interest does not mean they will not benefit from the relationship—they will. But it does mean that you must be fully informed on how professionals are to be compensated for their services. Two situations in which you should question an advisor's loyalty and independence are when you are referred from one professional to another and when all the professionals are employed by the same organization.

If a professional advisor refers you to another professional advisor with an understanding between them that the first will be paid part of the second advisor's fee, then the first advisor is required to inform you of this relationship. Payments of this kind are "kickbacks" and are absolutely unethical unless done with your express understanding and approval. For example, if an attorney or accountant referred you to a financial planner who was promoting tax-sheltered investments and if that attorney or accountant in any way shared in the fees paid to the financial planner, either directly or through the sale of an investment product, the law requires that you be advised of this financial arrangement. Therefore, when you are referred from one professional to another, do not hesitate to inquire whether there is any financial relationship between the two of them.

The second situation in which advisors may not be truly independent is when they are all part of the same corporation or partnership retained by you to perform financial and estate-planning services. These organizations offer the advantage of one-stop, comprehensive, and total financial and estate-planning services. They have as a part of the organization an attorney, an accountant, pension consultants, and a variety of investment advisors who are alleged to have experience in virtually every conceivable kind of asset in which you might invest.

Each of these individuals is basically an employee of the organization, which usually operates under a name such as The Corporation for Everyone's Complete, Total, and Final Investment and Estate-Planning Services. Each of these individuals will share in the fees you pay to the organization. They will also share in the profits of the organization, which many times are the result of its commissions from the various types of investment products purchased by you, the client.

These organizations often offer to provide a financial analysis and prepare drafts of wills and trusts and pension plans at substantially reduced fees. What they seek, of course, is control of your money and investments because the commissions on the sale of investment products are so great.

What you surrender in this kind of relationship is the independence of any one advisor. No one is going to rock the boat. No one will question any other advisor's conclusions and recommendations. It is not in their financial interest to do so.

Doing your investment and estate planning through one of these organizations can be cheap but very expensive— expensive because your interest is subordinated to that of the organization. Furthermore, it is often difficult to extricate yourself from the entanglements of such an organization should you become dissatisfied. If this occurs, you will find an attitude and degree of cooperation far different than when you became involved.

Understanding and appreciating the roles of the various investment and estate-planning advisors is essential. To what extent you choose to rely on them is an individual decision. If you do not have a good feeling about their recommendations, although you may like them personally, you should move with caution. This is a judgment call on your part, and regardless of how highly recommended they may be, you should be guided by your own intuition.

Common Sense

We make a living by what we get,
but we make a life by what we give.
Winston Churchill

Good investment planning and estate planning recognize the limitations inherent in all planning. Plans are not guarantees. They require effort, commitment, and constant revision to meet changes in the economy, in our relationships, and in our own changing desires and objectives.

Providing for the disposition of our assets upon death can be fraught with frustration. Attempts to control beyond our death the future of individuals and institutions who survive us can be senseless. But rarely are we prepared to confront the limitations of our mortality.

Heirs are often ill prepared to deal with their benefactor's largess. George Gilder in a talk before the American College of Probate Counsel described this all-too-common problem when he said, "The ingenuity of heirs in ridding themselves of their wealth is usually equal to the ingenuity of their forebears who created it." This is indeed a cruel irony for a lifetime of sacrifice and planning.

Keeping goals in a proper perspective is essential to good planning. Shaped by our values, tempered by our experiences, investment planning and estate planning are, in the final analysis, an expression of our faith in ourselves—our wisdom, our judgment, and most of all our common sense.

Index